Elite • 260

The German Navy 1935–45

The *Kriegsmarine* in World War II

NIGEL THOMAS PhD

ILLUSTRATED BY JOHNNY SHUMATE

Series editors Martin Windrow & Nick Reynolds

OSPREY PUBLISHING
Bloomsbury Publishing plc
Kemp House, Chawley Park, Cumnor Hill, Oxford OX2 9PH, UK
29 Earlsfort Terrace, Dublin 2, Ireland
1385 Broadway, Fifth Floor, New York, NY 10018, USA
E-mail: info@ospreypublishing.com
www.ospreypublishing.com

OSPREY is a trademark of Osprey Publishing Ltd

First published in Great Britain in 2025

A catalogue record for this book is available from the British Library

ISBN: PB: 9781472863126; eBook: 9781472863133; ePDF: 9781472863102;
XML: 9781472863119

25 26 27 28 29   10 9 8 7 6 5 4 3 2 1

Editor: Martin Windrow
Index by Angela Hall
Typeset by PDQ Digital Solutions, Bungay, UK
Printed by Repro India Ltd.

Acknowledgements

Nigel Thomas would like to thank Christopher Harrod for his interest,
generosity and patience during the preparation of this book. He also
expresses his particular gratitude to his son Dominick for his tireless
encouragement and support; and wishes to acknowledge the published
work of the following:
John R. Angolia, Chris Bishop, Helmut Blocksdorf, Wolfgang Böhler, Bernd
Bölscher, Vladimir Brnardić, Brian Leigh Davis, Eduardo Delgado, Lars
Hellwinkel, Bodo Herzog, Sigurd Henner, Thomas L. Houlihan III, Eberhard
Hettler, David Littlejohn, Jak P. Mallmann-Showell, Thomas McGuirl, Chris
McNab, Jamie Prenatt, Guido Rosignoli, John Russell, Adolf Schlicht, Mark
Stille, Georg Tessin, Gordon Williamson, Josef Zienert and Georg Zivkovic.

For further information on Nigel Thomas or to contact him, please refer to
his website: nt-associates.com

Editor's note

For reasons of space, this text employs abbreviations which vary from
normal house style.

Title page photo

May 1941: aboard U-129, *Admiral* Eugen Lindau, commanding MGK *West*
(left) welcomes *Kapitänleutnant* Asmus Clausen (right) and his watch
officers to *2. U-Flottille's* base at Lorient on France's Atlantic coast. This Type
IXC boat was commissioned that March, so is presumably returning from its
first patrol. The officers sport 'deep sea' beards, but *KL* Clausen does not
wear the boat-commander's traditional white cap-cover. (Admiral Lindau
(Lorient). JPG Wikimedia Commons)

Abbreviations & translations

AA	anti-aircraft		MAR	Naval Arty Rgt
AT	anti-tank		MEA	Naval Replacement Bn
MGK	Naval Group Command		MFA	Naval AA Bn
MOK	Naval Senior Command		NCO	non-commissioned officer
Abteilung	detachment or battalion		NSDAP	Nazi Party
Arty	artillery		OKM	Naval Supreme HQ
Bn	battalion		OKW	Armed Forces Supreme HQ
Coy / Coys	company / ies		RAD	German Labour Service
FOC	Flag Officer Commanding		RAF	Royal Air Force (British)
HMS	His Majesty's Ship (British RN)		Rgt	regiment
Inf	infantry		RN	Royal Navy (British)
K.i.a.	killed in action		SK	Naval District
MAA	Naval Arty Bn		SKL	Naval Warfare Command

CONTENTS

SUMMARY: CAMPAIGNS   4

Spain, 1936–39 ▪ Surface operations, 1939–45 ▪ German naval lineage ▪ Submarine operations
German Minesweeping Administration, 1945–48 ▪ Merchant Navy

NAVAL ORGANIZATION   14

North Sea & Baltic Sea 'Stations'/ Naval Group Commands ▪ Regional organization: Flag Officers
Commanding/ Sea Commanders

THE GERMAN FLEET, 1939–45   17

Surface ships: Ships-of-the-line ▪ Capital ships ▪ Cruisers ▪ Destroyers ▪ Auxiliary cruisers
Torpedo boats ▪ Speed boats ▪ Anti-mine, anti-submarine, patrol & security vessels ▪ Submarines
Special forces ▪ Naval aviation

NAVAL LAND FORCES   32

Naval Infantry ▪ Naval Artillery ▪ Naval Anti-Aircraft Artillery ▪ Other land branches
Foreign volunteers ▪ Foreign guard units

UNIFORMS   42

Navy-blue uniforms ▪ White uniforms ▪ Brown uniforms ▪ Fatigue uniforms ▪ Field-grey uniforms

RANKS & RANK INSIGNIA   50

BRANCH INSIGNIA   54

OTHER INSIGNIA   60

Trade badges ▪ War badges ▪ Combat clasps & badges ▪ Campaign shields ▪ Cuff titles

INDEX   64

THE GERMAN NAVY 1935–45

SUMMARY: CAMPAIGNS

Spain, 1936–39

The first armed action by the *Kriegsmarine* was its intervention in the Spanish Civil War (17 July 1936–1 Apr 1939), in support of the Nationalist Gen Francisco Franco's forces against those of the Spanish Republic. In Nov 1936 the German Navy sent a first 13-man advisory group; the subsequent North Sea Group (*Gruppe Nordsee*), with 34 instructors, remained with the Nationalist Navy until Mar 1939. A total of 35 German warships were

also rotated on missions in the Atlantic Ocean and Mediterranean Sea: 3 'pocket battleships' (super-heavy cruisers), 6 light cruisers, the 2nd Torpedo-Boat Flotilla (12 boats), and 14 submarines. Their patrols ostensibly enforced the League of Nations non-intervention agreement, but in reality supported Franco.[1]

Surface operations, 1939–45

On 27 Jan 1939 Hitler ordered the expansion of the Navy under Plan Z, to comprise new battleships, heavy cruisers and aircraft carriers. Unsurprisingly, only minimal work had been achieved by the outbreak of World War II on 1 Sept 1939, and in practice priority was given to expanding Admiral Dönitz's submarine fleet. The 'battle of Westerplatte' in Danzig harbour (now Gdańsk, Poland) on the first day of World War II saw the old pre-World War I ship-of-the-line *Schleswig Holstein* shelling the Polish Army garrison.

Generaladmiral Raeder, the naval Commander-in-Chief, identified Britain's large Royal Navy as his principal enemy. On 13 Dec 1939 in the Western Atlantic, an RN squadron forced the damaged commerce-raiding 'pocket battleship' *Admiral Graf Spee*, commanded by *Kapitän zur See* Hans

---

1 See also Elite 131, *The Condor Legion*.

Langsdorff, to take shelter in Montevideo on the River Plate estuary between neutral Argentina and Uruguay. Rather than risk renewing the battle against a reportedly reinforced enemy, Langsdorff scuttled *Graf Spee* and committed suicide. The outcome of this Battle of the River Plate, the first major naval encounter of World War II, was a welcome encouragement for the Allies. German and British submarines and destroyers undertook operations on both sides of the North Sea during Jan and Feb 1940.

From 27 Jan 1940 the Germans planned an invasion of neutral Norway to secure strategic Swedish iron ore supplies passing through Narvik. On 16 Feb an RN destroyer crew provocatively boarded the German supply-ship *Altmark* in Norwegian waters to free prisoners taken earlier from merchantmen by *Graf Spee*, and Hitler ordered the planned invasion to go ahead. This formed part of Operation '*Weserübung*' (which also violated a non-aggression pact with Denmark), and involved a dangerous North Sea crossing – the largest German amphibious operation of World War II. From 7 Apr 1940 six naval groups (*Gruppen* I–VI) transported German Army units to separate landing sites, evading RN Home Fleet elements which were distracted by hunting for the German capital ships. On 9 Apr the cruiser *Blücher* was sunk in Oslofjord by the Norwegian coastal battery at Drøbak Sound; the RN and its Fleet Air Arm then defeated the German Navy in two battles on 10 and 13 Apr, sinking several destroyers and the cruiser *Königsberg* (the first major warship ever to be sunk by aircraft). British, French and Free Polish troops landing from 14 Apr had some initial success in ground fighting around Narvik, but were quite outclassed by the smaller German Army landing force with its *Luftwaffe* support. On 8 June the Allied troops were forced to evacuate to Britain and to France, where the German *Blitzkrieg* campaign had opened on 10 May. On 10 June Norway surrendered after 62 days' resistance, but the German Navy, which had lost ten destroyers and three cruisers, regarded the Norwegian campaign as a defeat.

German naval participation in the battle of France was limited due to the superior strength of Allied warships in the English Channel, culminating in the British evacuation from Dunkirk in May–June 1940. Hitler planned an invasion of Britain (Operation '*Seelöwe*') for Sept 1940, but Raeder was pessimistic about facing the RN in the Channel, and the *Luftwaffe's* failure to defeat the Royal Air Force in the Battle of Britain (10 July–31 Oct 1940) forced a permanent postponement of this always controversial plan. Germany gained a numerically strong but unreliable ally on 10 June 1940, when Mussolini's Fascist Italy opportunistically declared war on Britain and France. The German occupation of Norway, Denmark, the Netherlands, Belgium, and especially France in June 1940 allowed the

OPPOSITE

France, 1942: this leading seaman is among submarine crewmen being awarded medals; for the parade, he wears the M1933 peakless navy-blue sailors' cap. His pea-jacket bears cornflower-blue collar patches with his single gold braid rank bar and braid collar edging, and a gold-wire breast eagle. It was fairly common for NCOs and even ratings to display superior-quality private purchase versions of insignia. Despite his modest rank this submariner has already been awarded both classes of the Iron Cross (2nd Class ribbon bar, and pinback 1st Class badge on his left breast, above the U-Boat War Badge). He has just been presented with the German Cross in Silver (right breast); instituted on 28 Sept 1941, this was second only to the Knight's Cross. (Bundesarchiv, Bild 101II-MW-3491-06, Buchheim Lothar-Günther / CC-BY-SA 3.0 / Wikimedia Commons)

German Navy thereafter to deploy destroyers, torpedo-boats, submarines and the formidable battleships *Bismarck* and *Tirpitz* from French ports, to threaten the RN and British merchant shipping in the Channel and the North Atlantic as well as the North Sea.

In the Atlantic, on 24 May 1941 the battleship HMS *Hood* was sunk by *Bismarck* and *Prinz Eugen*, followed by the engagement of an RN task force which defeated and forced the scuttling of *Bismarck* on 27 May. This proved that even the most powerful German warships were potentially vulnerable to combined naval and air attacks on the high seas, prompting Raeder to protect most of his operational strength at anchor in home waters and the captured harbours of western France.

In Feb 1941 the *Kriegsmarine* initiated its Mediterranean campaign in support of Italy, attacking Allied supply shipping to North Africa supported by the *Luftwaffe;* this campaign was extended in April 1941 to the Adriatic and Aegean Seas, and, from Germany's invasion of the USSR on 21 June 1941, into the Black Sea. The most costly, though ultimately successful Allied convoys were those to re-supply the besieged island of Malta, a base for British submarines and aircraft, during 27 June 1940–31 Dec 1943. Germany made extensive use of its torpedo-boats in this theatre, in concert with successful Italian special attack units. The Russian Front was primarily a land war, but the German and Finnish navies operated in the Baltic Sea and the *Kriegsmarine* to a lesser extent in the Black Sea.

In 1942 there was increased naval activity in the English Channel. In the so-called 'Channel Dash' of 11–13 Feb *Vizeadmiral* Ciliax, with heavy air support, successfully led a large squadron including *Gneisenau, Scharnhorst* and *Prinz Eugen* from Brest in Brittany up into the Channel and eastwards all the way to Wilhelmshaven, fighting off RN and RAF attacks. There were other Channel convoys (e.g. one led successfully by the auxiliary cruiser

A **EARLY OPERATIONS**

(A1) *Fregattenkapitän*; Wilhelmshaven, Sept 1939
This senior-grade commander of the Line branch wears navy-blue walking-out dress with grey leather gloves. His cap peak shows senior officers' gold-wire oakleaf edging, as introduced on 1 July 1936. The eagle-and-swastika insignia above the gold-wreathed cockade on his cap, and the larger version on his right breast, are both hand-embroidered in gold wire. Beneath the Line star on the sleeves of the service dress tunic, the four medium-depth gold lace cuff-rings of this rank will be changed to three on 1 Aug 1940, and finally, on 25 Feb 1944, to one medium/ one narrow/ two medium (top to bottom). This officer displays the pinback Iron Cross 1st Class breast badge and the buttonhole ribbon of the preliminary 2nd Class.

(A2) *Obermaschinenmaat*; Aviso 'Grille', Aug 1939
This senior leading seaman engineer serves on the *Aviso 'Grille'* (Despatch Boat 'Cricket'), which served as Hitler's state yacht in 1935–39, and wears the junior NCOs' peacetime summer walking-out dress. The white-covered peakless sailors' cap bears the eagle and cockade insignia introduced on 15 Mar 1933, and the vessel's name in gold Gothic script on the black 'tally' ribbon. He wears a white summer jumper, with the wide light blue sailors' collar and black silk scarf folded out over the short '*Affenjacke*' parade jacket. This has two linked gold anchor-embossed front buttons between two rows of eight, and five on the cuffs, which also bear vertical and horizontal NCO braid. In addition to the Navy breast eagle, the jacket displays on the right sleeve the Führer's flag, and on the left the Engineer ratings' branch badge of a cogwheel on an anchor with a miniature seniority chevron, above the red trade badge indicating qualification as an *Unterwasserhorcher* sonar operator (a downward arrow against waves).

(A3) *Hauptfeldwebel*, 121st Naval Artillery Battalion; Laboe, Sept 1939
This chief petty officer's appointment as a company sergeant-major in his Land Forces unit is indicated by the double yellow NCO-braid cuff rings on the M1935 field-grey service tunic, and his bulging black leather report book. The peaked-cap band and piping are dark green, as are the tunic collar and the pointed shoulder straps; both the collar and straps are edged with yellow NCO braid. The shoulder straps bear two 4-point silver rank stars and the initial branch badge of gold crossed-anchors, but unit numbers were ordered removed from early in 1939 for security reasons. The breast eagle is worked in gold wire on dark green backing. The dark green collar patches bear matt grey *Litzen* 'Guard bars' with yellow centre-stripes. The belt has the M1936 Navy yellow-metal buckle-plate. At this date the grey trousers contrasted with the field-grey colour of the tunic.

Konteradmiral Hubert Schmundt commanded a squadron of the Bergen Group in the invasion of Norway, Apr 1940, and subsequently naval forces in the Baltic 1943-44, but he was dismissed from service in Apr 1944. Here he wears flag officers' service dress; note the double row of gold oakleaf embroidery on his cap peak, and his cuff ranking of one gold medium ring above one deep ring, below the star identifying Line officers. His awards include the Knight's Cross (14 June 1940); the silver eagle with '1939' clasp indicating both World War I and World War II awards of the Iron Cross 2nd Class; the Iron Cross 1st Class; and the Minesweeper War Badge. (KAdm Schmundt.jpg / Wikimedia Commons)

Michel on 14 Mar 1942), but as the year drew on such exploits became less viable as the RN and RAF grew in strength.

For their part, between Aug 1941 and May 1945 the Allies ran 78 Arctic merchant convoys carrying military hardware and supplies from the USA, Canada, and Britain across the Atlantic and Arctic oceans to Arkhangelsk and Murmansk in the far northern Soviet Union (USSR). These convoys past the long Norwegian coast ran the gauntlet of attacks by the *Kriegsmarine* and *Luftwaffe*, and even the perceived threat of interception by German capital ships could have tragic consequences. However, the inconclusive Battle of the Barents Sea (31 Dec 1942) prompted an exasperated Hitler

to limit the operations of major surface warships. This led Raeder to resign on 30 Jan 1943; he was given the operationally irrelevant appointment of *Admiralinspektor*, while Dönitz was promoted *Großadmiral* and Navy Commander-in-Chief. Since Dönitz's appointment came only days before the catastrophic German Army surrender at Stalingrad, he inherited supreme naval command just as Germany's fortunes began a slow but continuous decline.

Naval activity from Jan to Oct 1943 was increasingly dominated by small local actions, with security ships ensuring the passage of German convoys and submarines along Channel sea-lanes, in the Bay of Biscay and coastal waters, while the large surface ships remained vulnerable to Allied attack. On land, 1943 proved disastrous to Germany, with the loss of North Africa (13 May) and Sicily (10 July), and defeat by the Red Army at Kursk (4–13 July). The surrender of Italy on 8 Sept robbed Germany of a numerically strong (if seldom energetic) naval ally. The Allies now dominated the Mediterranean, although the Germans managed to remain effective in the Aegean Sea.

Some torpedo-boats resisted the Allied landings in Normandy on 6 June 1944, sinking one destroyer, but Allied strengths at sea, in the air and on the ground were now so overwhelmingly superior that the Germans were forced out of France in October. (Finally, after several failed attempts, on 12 Nov 1944 RAF Lancaster bombers sank the *Tirpitz*, Germany's most powerful surviving warship, in its Norwegian anchorage.) By Jan 1945 German naval resources were disastrously diminished, but they fought on by sea and on land as well as they were able.

As the Red Army advanced into East Prussia in Jan 1945 Dönitz actioned Operation 'Hannibal', the mass evacuation of German troops and civilians from Courland, East Prussia, West Prussia and Pomerania to western Germany and Denmark. Over 15 weeks from 23 Jan 1945, about 2 million Germans were evacuated by *Admiral* Conrad Kummetz's fleet of 22 ocean liners, about 1,080 merchantmen and fishing vessels, and what remained of the German Navy – the largest such operation in history, dwarfing the Dunkirk evacuation of 1940. The former liner *Wilhelm Gustloff*, operating as

The battleship *Bismarck* was Germany's most formidable warship (see Osprey Campaign 232, *The Bismarck 1941*). Its sinking on 24 May 1941 of Britain's newest battleship, HMS *Hood* – in a few minutes, and with virtually all hands – shocked the Royal Navy and the British public. It led to an unprecedented North Atlantic chase by an RN task force, leading to *Bismarck's* complete disablement and final scuttling on 27 May. (Bundesarchiv Bild 193-04-1-26 / CC-BY-SA 3.0 / Wikimedia Commons)

a hospital ship, was transporting about 10,000 German troops and civilians on 30 Jan 1945 when it was torpedoed and sunk by LtCdr Aleksandr I. Marinesko's Red Navy Baltic Fleet submarine S-13 off the Pomeranian coast. The resultant loss of some 9,300 lives was the highest casualty count from any single ship in maritime history.

SUBMARINE OPERATIONS

On 27 Sept 1935 the first German post-1918 submarine (sing. *Unterseeboot / U-Boot*; plur. *Unterseeboote/ U-Boote*) was launched, and on 1 Oct 1939 *Kapitän zur See* Karl Dönitz was promoted *Konteradmiral* and appointed Commander of Submarines (*Befehlshaber der Unterseeboote*). Initially, submarines were forbidden to attack unescorted merchant ships without prior warning, but from Feb 1940 any vessel was fair game. The conquest of France allowed Dönitz's submarines to operate from heavily fortified flotilla bases on the French Atlantic coast and, to a lesser extent, from Aug 1941 they were able to harry the Arctic convoys from Norway.

From June 1940 onwards the *U-Boote* enjoyed significant success against the RN and merchant shipping along Britain's transatlantic lifeline, prompting their crews to name this period 'the Happy Time'. Between Feb and Dec 1941 the fleet's strength rose from 103 to 247 boats, notwithstanding 38 losses. The US Navy's neglect of effective convoy tactics along their East Coast after their entry into the war in December brought Germany's submariners a 'Second Happy Time' in Jan to Aug 1942. Instead of individual patrols, from 1941 U-boats increasingly operated in large coordinated groups called 'wolf-packs' (sing., *Rudel),* which could wreak havoc among Allied merchant convoys and their escorts. Boat commanders attacked more often on the surface by night than when submerged by day; the increasing minority who achieved five sinkings were dubbed 'aces', and given celebrity status in the German media. At the end of 1942 U-boat strength was 397; losses that year had totalled 88, the worst month being October, with 16 boats sunk.

Although Dönitz's strength peaked at 447 boats in January 1944, during 1943 the tide of the submarine war turned against Germany, due to Allied intelligence intercepted from the German 'Enigma' coding machine; enhanced Allied aerial surveillance over the mid-Atlantic 'gap'; growing radar capability in locating boats on the surface; and improved anti-submarine weapons.

This rating, sporting a moustache and closely-trimmed beard, is wearing a navy-blue peakless sailors' cap with a customized wide crown, the gilt metal eagle-and-swastika above the tricolour cockade and the wartime *'Kriegsmarine'* cap-tally. Another departure from regulations is the black leather shoulder reinforcement evidently added to his *Uberzieher* pea-jacket. (Bundesarchiv Bild 101II-MN-1589-23 / Mendel / CC-BY-SA 3.0 / Wikimedia Commons)

During 1943 Dönitz lost 245 boats, and 42 in May 1943 alone, which forced him to withdraw from the Atlantic convoy lanes. Thereafter his boat commanders were more often the hunted than the hunters, and Germany had effectively lost the 'Battle of the Atlantic'.

During the war a total of 32 U-boats operated in the Baltic, and from Aug 1941 submarines were also deployed in the 'Battle of the Arctic', with a peak of 23 boats in Dec 1942. From Sept 1941 a total of 65 U-boats operated in the Mediterranean against British naval and supply shipping, using Italian and clandestine Spanish port facilities, but this became increasingly costly even before Italy's surrender in Sept 1943. From June 1942 half-a-dozen boats operated in the Black Sea against Soviet ships supporting the Red Army in the Caucasus and Ukraine. However, on 23 Aug and 9 Sept 1944 respectively, Romania and Bulgaria both capitulated to the Soviet Union, and remaining U-boats were scuttled in Turkish waters.

Japan formed the Tripartite Pact with Germany and Italy on 27 Sept 1940. From Mar 1942 German submarines successfully attacked Allied shipping in the South Atlantic off Africa. From Oct 1942 a total of 29 boats reached the Indian Ocean, establishing repair bases beginning with Penang in 1943, followed by Singapore, Jakarta, Surabaya, and even in Kobe, Japan. Some modified *Milchkuh* ('milk-cow') U-boats even transported fuel to the Imperial Japanese Navy in 1944–45.

The U-boats were unable to resist the Allied landings in Normandy and the South of France in June and Aug 1944 respectively, and by the latter month the submarine fleet's days as a significant force were numbered, with only two bases still operational in Norway and three in Germany. In

The *Wilhelm Gustloff* at anchor in Danzig, 1940. Launched in 1937, this cruise liner served from Sept 1939 to Nov 1940 as a hospital ship in the Baltic Sea and Norwegian waters, before becoming a floating barracks for the 2nd Submarine Training Division. On 30 Jan 1945 during Operation 'Hannibal', the massive evacuation of German troops and civilians from threatened Prussia and Pomerania to western Germany and Denmark, it was sunk by a Red Navy submarine; this resulted in the greatest-ever loss of life from a single ship – c.9,300 of roughly 10,000 aboard. (Bundesarchiv Bild 183-H27992, Lazarettschiff "Wilhelm Gustloff" in Danzig. jpg / Wikimedia Commons)

France, although the German garrisons in Lorient, La Rochelle / La Pallice and St Nazaire held out, pointlessly, until May 1945, their boats had long been withdrawn or scuttled. The production of advanced classes of *U-Boote* continued in small numbers, and they remained a rare threat until the very end, but the frequency of their patrols had decreased enormously.

On 30 Apr 1945 Adolf Hitler committed suicide, appointing *Großadmiral* Dönitz his successor as *Führer*. Dönitz ordered Germany's unconditional surrender to the Allies on 8 May 1945, though on paper he remained President (*Präsident*) of Germany and Commander of the Armed Forces (*Oberbefehlshaber der Wehrmacht*) until his 'Flensburg Cabinet' was officially dissolved on 5 June. At the Nuremberg Trials (20 Nov 1945–1 Oct 1946) Raeder was sentenced to life imprisonment, subsequently reduced to ten years, for war crimes and waging a war of aggression; he was released in 1955 and died on 6 Nov 1960. Dönitz was also sentenced to ten years, living thereafter until 24 Dec 1980.

German Minesweeping Administration, 1945–48

The German Navy was officially disbanded on 22 June 1945, and the surrendered surface and submarine fleets were transferred to Allied and other foreign navies. The previous day the British Military Government in Berlin had officially established the German Minesweeping Administration (GMSA), to clear about 600,000 naval mines from the North and Baltic Seas. The victorious Allies preferred to use German personnel for this dangerous work rather than their own; commanded by RN Cdre H. T. England, with

Konteradmiral Fritz Krauß, wartime commander of German minesweepers, as the senior German officer, the GMSA deployed some 27,000 former German minesweeping personnel in about 300 vessels. Being classed as Disarmed Enemy Forces, they initially wore regulation *Kriegsmarine* uniforms with the eagle-and-swastika removed. On 25 May 1946 new uniforms were introduced, comprising RN navy-blue battledress with a peaked field cap or peakless on-board cap. The GMSA was formed into 1st–6th Mine Clearance Divisions (*Räumbootdivisionen*) with HQ at Glückstadt, transferring to Hamburg in December 1947. Under Soviet pressure this organization, which enjoyed high morale, was disbanded in Jan 1948, having lost 348 officers and men.

The US Office of the Military Government established the parallel Navy Service Group (*Marine-Dienstgruppe* – MDG) at Bremerhaven from June 1945 to Dec 1947. This too wore wartime uniform with the Nazi national emblem removed. It undertook both minesweeping duties and the repair of 100 German Navy vessels for transfer to Allied navies or merchant navies.

Merchant Navy

All commercial shipping of the German Merchant Navy (*Deutsche Handelsmarine*) was controlled by the Reich Ministry of Transport. Upon mobilization on 26 Aug 1939 merchantmen came under Navy control. Personnel served on merchant ships and Navy minesweepers, submarine-hunters and security vessels, qualifying where appropriate for the Minesweeper and Blockade-Runner war badges. Merchant Navy officers wore a navy-blue peaked cap with a wreathed cockade badge, and a double-

The U-boat's deck gun was often used against isolated merchant ships, and the wider deck of the Type IX boats allowed the mounting of a more powerful 10.5cm gun in place of the Type VII's 8.8cm. This shows the guncrew of the Type IXB boat U-123 (*2. U-Flottille*) during Feb 1942; note the dark and light shades of grey paint used on the gun's top and side surfaces respectively. Commissioned on 30 May 1940, U-123 was scuttled at Lorient on 17 June 1944 following the Normandy landings. Recovered, it was later recommissioned by the French Navy as the submarine *Blaison*. (Bundesarchiv, Bild 101II-MW-4006-31 / Tölle / CC-BY-SA 3.0 / Wikimedia Commons)

breasted service tunic with cuff rank-rings. Ratings wore a navy-blue uniform with a brass eagle-and-swastika or a shipping-line cap-badge above a gold-edged ribbon tally bearing 'Deutsche Handelsmarine' in gold.

NAVAL ORGANIZATION

The German Navy's organization was extremely complex and in constant flux, arguably more so than for the numerically much larger German Army. Limited space therefore allows only a brief summary here.

The Naval Supreme Command (*Oberkommando der Kriegsmarine* – OKM) was controlled by the Commander-in-Chief of the Navy *(Oberbefehlshaber der Kriegsmarine)*: from 1 June 1935, *Generaladmiral* (later *Großadmiral*) Erich Raeder; 30 Jan 1943, *Großadmiral* Karl Dönitz; 1 May 1945, *Generaladmiral* Hans-Georg von Friedeburg; 23 May–22 July 1945, *Generaladmiral* Walter Warzecha. The C-in-C reported personally to Hitler. Directly subordinate to the OKM was the Naval Warfare Command (*Seekriegsleitung* – SKL), re-established in 1937 to control sea operations, with six operational and administrative departments, including the Fleet Command *(Flottenkommando)* responsible for all naval vessels. Various types of ships were divided under independent sub-departments.

KL Hans Bartels was awarded the Knight's Cross on 16 May 1940 as commander of Minesweeper M-1, and in Aug 1944 led 261. *K-Flot* of the *K-Verbände* special forces, with *Biber* one-man submersibles. Joining the German Minesweeping Administration after VE-Day, he died in an accident on 31 July 1945. (Bundesarchiv Bild 146-2006-0124, Hans Bartels / Wikimedia Commons)

North Sea & Baltic Sea 'Stations'/ Naval Group Commands

The German coast was divided from 19 May 1870 into two Naval Stations: North Sea (*Marinestation der Nordsee*), HQ Wilhelmshaven, and Baltic Sea (*Marinestation der Ostsee*), HQ Kiel. From 1938 the stations were gradually reorganized into Naval Senior Commands (*Marine*

B **ATLANTIC FRONT, 1941–43**

(B1) *Signaloberstabsgefreiter; Norway, July 1941*
This senior able seaman is wearing the ratings' navy-blue landing dress, comprising a jumper worn with the light blue sailors' collar and black scarf, and trousers with black leather short-shaft marching boots. The M1935 Army helmet, painted matt field-grey, had a decal of a yellow folded-wing *Wehrmacht* eagle on a black shield on the left side (abolished 17 July 1941), and a black-white-red diagonally striped national shield on the right (abolished 28 Aug 1943). This rating wears an M1934 yellow breast eagle machine-woven on navy-blue backing on his right breast. On his left upper arm he displays the yellow metal naval version of the M1940 Narvik campaign shield; a yellow, white and red crossed-flags Signals branch badge; a yellow star and two chevrons of rank; and below that a Level 2 motor engineer's trade badge. His belt and supporting Y-straps carry M1911 triple ammunition pouches on each front hip, and the bayonet scabbard on his left. Slung behind him are a gas-mask canister, and the standard 7.92mm *Karabiner 98k* bolt-action rifle.

(B2) *Oberleutnant zur See; France, July 1943*
This junior officer of the Line branch wears the navy-blue service dress with greatcoat. His cap peak has narrow gold-braid embroidery with a 'wavy' inner edge, introduced 1 July 1936. His greatcoat has deep turnback cuffs; its flat silver-wire cord shoulder straps on navy-blue underlay show one 4-point gold rank star, but no branch badge for Line personnel. For service ashore he wears navy-blue riding breeches with black riding boots. The white metal 6 x 30 binoculars were typically used by junior officers and senior NCOs.

(B3) *Marineartilleriefeldwebel*, **681st Light Artillery Battalion; France, June 1942**
This Naval Artillery petty officer wears the M1935 NCOs' field-grey service uniform, with an M1942 field cap. The latter has a yellow eagle machine-woven on field-grey on the crown, and on the flap a point-up-yellow piping chevron encloses the cockade. The tunic has a dark green collar and the field-grey shoulder straps introduced in 1940, both edged with yellow NCO braid. The shoulder straps bear the winged anchor branch badge introduced on 13 Mar 1939. This NCO displays the Iron Cross 2nd Class buttonhole ribbon, the Bronze Wound Badge (reintroduced 1 Sept 1939 for 1–2 wounds), and the Coastal Artillery War Badge instituted on 24 June 1941. He carries a P08 pistol at his left hip.

Oberkommandos – MOKs) comprising four Naval Group Commands (*Marinegruppenkommandos* – MGKs):

MGK Ost (East), formed 1 Nov 1938, HQ Kiel, controlling the Baltic Sea. It was redesignated *MGK Nord* (North) on 10 Aug 1940, HQ Wilhelmshaven, covering also the German Bight, Denmark, Norway and North Sea. Abolished 20 Oct 1944.

MGK West, formed Aug 1939, HQ Wilhelmshaven, controlling the North Sea; Aug 1940 transferred to Paris, covering France; abolished 20 Oct 1944. North Sea Naval Station was part of this MGK Aug 1940–July 1944, and Baltic Sea Naval Station Aug 1940–July 1944.

MGK Italien (Italy); formed Nov 1941, controlling the Mediterranean, Adriatic and Aegean Seas. It cooperated with the Royal Italian Navy until Italy's surrender on 8 Sept 1943; abolished Jan 1945.

MGK Süd (South); formed 30 July 1941, HQ Sofia (Bulgaria) until Aug 1944, controlling the Balkans, Black, Adriatic and Aegean Seas. Abolished 30 Dec 1944.

Regional organization

The two MOKs and four MGKs were divided into 15 admirals' 'Flag Officer Commanding' Naval Regions (listed alphabetically in **bold** below). These controlled about 68 subordinate Naval Districts under officers designated 'Sea Defence Commanders' or 'Sea Commanders' (*Kommandanten der Seeverteidigung* – *Seekommandanten* / SK) Apr 1940–8 May 1945 (as listed below). Ports were commanded by Sea Commanders; larger ports (with an attached Port Protection Flotilla) by a Port Commander (*Hafenkommandant*), and smaller ports by a Port Captain (*Hafenkapitän*).

Adm. Adriatic Sea: SK Albania, SK Dalmatia (later SK N. Dalmatia and SK S. Dalmatia), SK North Adriatic (later SK Istria), SK West Adriatic.

Adm. Aegean Sea: SK L, later SK Volos, then SK Attica), SK S (later SK Crete), SK Dodecanese, SK N. Greece (from Salonika and Lemnos), SK Pelloponese, SK N (later SK Salonika, then SK N. Greece), SK W. Greece.

Adm. Atlantic Coast: SK Brest (later SK Brittany), SK Gascony, SK Loire, SK Vendée.

Adm. Black Sea: SK Romania, SK Crimea (previously Crimea-Ukraine), SK Caucasus (later SK Romania), SK V (later Ukraine), SK X (planned as SK Black Sea).

Adm. Channel Coast: SK Boulogne, SK Channel Islands, SK Pas de Calais, SK Dunkirk, SK Normandie, SK Ostende, SK Flanders (later SK Pas-de-Calais), SK Seine-Somme.

Großadmiral Erich Raeder wearing the flag officers' M1926 ceremonial dress, and holding his personalized baton of rank. Note the shirt's stiff white wing collar worn with a black bow-tie; the silver-braid ceremonial belt with a gilt metal 'anchor' clasp; and the grey kid-leather gloves. On the frock coat he uniquely wears shoulder straps of rank over the gold-lace retaining loops for epaulettes, and below his medals he displays the NSDAP's M1933 Gold Party Badge. This did not prevent Hitler from demoting him from Navy C-in-C to the largely ceremonial post of *Admiralinspektor* in Jan 1943. (Bundesarchiv Bild 146-1980-128-63, Erich Raeder. jpg / Wikimedia Commons)

Adm. Eastern Baltic: SK O (later SK Liepaja, then SK Latvia), SK R (later SK Estonia, then SK Baltic Islands), SK Q (later SK Tallinn), SK P (later SK Riga), SK East & West Prussia (later SK West Prussia).

Adm. German Bight: SK Elbe-Weser, SK North Frisia, SK East Frisia.

Adm. French South Coast: SK Loire (later SK Languedoc, then SK French Riviera), SK Italian Riviera, SK North Istria (later SK Istria).

Adm. Netherlands: SK Central Holland, SK N. Holland, SK S. Holland.

Adm. Norway North Coast: SK Molde, SK Sandnessjøen, SK Trondheim.

Adm. Norway Polar Coast: SK Hammerfest (later SK Harstad), SK Kirkenes, SK Narvik.

Adm. Norway: SK Oslo (later SK Oslofjord).

Adm. Norway South Coast (later **Norway West Coast**): SK Bergen, SK Polar Coast (later SK Tromsö), SK Kristiansand, SK Stavanger. SK R (intended for SK St Petersburg, later SK Estonia).

Adm. Skagerak: SK Danish Islands, SK N. Jutland, SK S. Jutland.

Adm. Western Baltic: SK Schleswig-Holstein-Mecklenburg (later Schleswig-Holstein), SK Pomerania.

THE GERMAN FLEET, 1939–45

SURFACE SHIPS

Ships-of-the-Line (sing., *Linienschiffe*) x 2

The *Schleswig-Holstein* and *Schlesien* were obsolete 'pre-dreadnought' warships commissioned in 1908. *Schleswig-Holstein* fired the first shots of World War II when it shelled the Polish Army at Westerplatte on 1 Sept 1939. It served in Danish and Norwegian waters in April 1940, but was mainly used as a training vessel thereafter. The *Schlesien* also served as a training ship, before ferrying refugees in Operation 'Hannibal', Jan–May 1945, from Gotenhafen (now Gdynia, Poland) to Swinemünde (now Świnoviście, Poland). It was scuttled there in shallow water on 4 May, although its AA guns remained operational.

Wilhelm Marschall photographed as a *Kapitän zur See* in 1936, wearing the officers' navy-blue service dress with greatcoat; note the naval officer's dress dagger hanging from an internal suspension, emerging from below the coat's left pocket-flap. At his throat he displays the prestigious *Pour le Mérite* cross which he had won on 4 July 1918 as a submarine commander. Marschall was promoted *Konteradmiral* in 1936, and would command the battleship *Gneisenau* in the Norwegian campaign, sinking the RN aircraft carrier HMS *Glorious* on 8 June 1940. He subsequently commanded MGK *West* from 21 Sept 1942 to 20 Apr 1943, being promoted *Generaladmiral* on 1 Feb 1943. (Bundesarchiv Bild 183-2008-0812-500/CC-BY-SA 3.0 / Wikimedia Commons)

The *Graf Zeppelin*, Germany's first and only aircraft carrier, was intended to be the jewel in the crown of Plan Z – the expansion of the *Kriegsmarine* into a force capable of challenging the Royal Navy. In the event, the outbreak of war on 1 Sept 1939 found the German Navy wholly unprepared to complete Plan Z, which was promptly abandoned. The *Graf Zeppelin* was launched incomplete at Kiel on 8 Dec 1938; never completed, it was eventually scuttled. Had it been commissioned, it was planned to carry a 42-strong air group: 10 Messerschmitt Bf 109T fighters, 12 Junkers Ju 87E dive-bombers, and 20 Fieseler Fi 167 torpedo-bombers. (Bundesarchiv, Bild 146-1982-145-29A, Flugzeugträger "Graf Zeppelin", Bau.jpg / Wikimedia Commons)

CAPITAL SHIPS

Battleships (*Schlachtschiffe*) x 4

The two Bismarck Class battleships were *Bismarck* and *Tirpitz*. *Bismarck* left Gotenhaven in May 1941 but was soon tracked in the North Atlantic by the Royal Navy; it sank HMS *Hood*, but was completely disabled and finally scuttled on 27 May. *Tirpitz* left Wilhelmshafen for Norwegian anchorages on 16 Jan 1942, but its only offensive action was the brief 'Spitsbergen Raid' of 8 Sept 1943. Surviving several failed air raids by the RN and RAF, it was damaged in Kaafjord on 22 Sept 1943 by RN X-Craft midget submarines, and was finally sunk by RAF Lancasters in Tromso Fjord on 12 Nov 1944.

In late 1939 the two Scharnhorst Class battleships *Scharnhorst* and *Gneisenau* carried out combined operations with *Admiral Hipper* against

---

TABLE 1: Selective battle order of surface ships, 1 Sept 1939–8 May 1945

2 Ships-of-the-Line: *Schlesien* (May 1908–May 1945); *Schleswig-Holstein* (July 1908–Jan 1945)
4 Battleships: *Bismarck* (Aug 1940–May 1941); *Tirpitz* (Feb 1941–Nov 1944); *Scharnhorst* (Jan 1939–Dec 1943); *Gneisenau* (May 1938– Feb 1942)
3 Super-heavy Cruisers ('pocket battleships'): *Deutschland* (Apr 1933–May 1945); *Admiral Scheer* (Nov 1934–Apr 1945); *Admiral Graf Spee* (Jan 1936–Dec 1939)
5 Heavy Cruisers: *Admiral Hipper* (Apr 1939–May 1945); *Blücher* (Sept 1939–Apr 1940); *Prinz Eugen* (Aug 1940–summer 1946); *Seydlitz* (Jan 1939–Apr 1945); *Lützow* (July 1939–Feb 1940)
6 Light Cruisers: *Emden* (Oct 1925–Apr 1945); *Königsberg* (Apr 1929–Apr 1940); *Karlsruhe* (Nov 1929–Apr 1940); *Köln* (Jan 1930–Mar 1945); *Leipzig* (Oct 1931–Dec 1946); *Nürnberg* (Nov 1935–Jan 1946)
1 Aircraft Carrier: *Graf Zeppelin* (Dec 1938–1945)

42 Destroyers
1. Flotilla: Z1–Z4, Z14–Z16 (Sept 1938–Apr 1940). **2. Flotilla:** Z1, Z5–Z8 (Sept 1938–May 1940). **3. Flotilla:** Z17–Z0, Z22 (Dec 1939–Apr 1940). **4. Flotilla:** Z9–Z13 (Apr 1939–Apr 1940); Z31–Z34, Z37–Z39 (Oct 1942–May 1945). **5. Flotilla:** Z2–Z4, Z14–Z6, ZH1 (May 1940–May 1945). **6. Flotilla:** Z5–Z8, Z10, Z20, Z35, Z36, Z43 (May 1940–May 1945). **8. Flotilla:** (Z23–Z30 (Dec 1940–Aug 1944; Nov 1944–May 1945)

11 Auxiliary Cruisers
HSK1 *Orion* (Dec 1939–May 1945); HSK2 *Atlantis* (Dec 1939–Nov 1941); HSK3 *Widder* (Dec 1939–Oct 1940); HSK4 *Thor* (May 1940–Nov 1942); HSK5 *Pinguin* (Sept 1939–May 1941); HSK5 (II) *Hansa* (Apr 1943–May 1945); HSK6 *Stier* (Apr 1941–Sept 1942); HSK7 *Komet* (1939–Oct 1942); HSK8 *Kormoran* (June 1940–Nov 1941); HSK9 *Michel* (Sept 1941–Oct 1943); *Coronel* (June 1940–May 1945)

109 Torpedo Boats
1. Flotilla: T1–T4, T9, T10 (Oct 1939 – Aug 1941); **2. Flotilla:** T1–T12 (Oct 1939–May 1945). **3. Flotilla:** T13–T21 (Apr 1941–May 1945). **4. Flotilla:** T22–T29 (Feb 1943–Apr 1944). **5. Flotilla:** *Albatros, Falke, Greif, Iltis, Jaguar, Kondor, Seeadler, Tiger, Möwe* (Sept 1939; later, T22–T25). **6. Flotilla** *Iltis, Jaguar, Leopard, Luchs, Wolf, Seeadler* (Sept 1939–Feb 1941; T28–T33, Nov 1943–Aug 1944). **7. Flotilla:** *Leopard, Löwe, Panther, Tiger* (June–Dec 1940). **9. Flotilla :** TA14–TA19 (Sept 1943–Oct 1944); TA40–TA45 (Feb–May 1945). **10. Flotilla:** TA23–TA33 (Jan 1944–May 1945)

170 Speed boats in 15 Flotillas
1. Speed Boat Div (3., 7., 21., 22. & 24. Flotillas) (July 1943–May 1945); **1., 2., 4.–6., 8.–11. & 24. Flotillas**

1939: the crew of a Type 1938 (S14 Class) *Schnellboot* load a 53.3cm torpedo for the port tube. Armament on *S-boote* varied widely, increasing throughout the war, particularly in AA weapons. This particular class had only four boats, numbered S-14 to S-17, with stern armament of a single 20mm cannon. S-17 was lost due to storm damage in 1939. S-14 sank in the Channel in 1944; later recovered, it proved to be beyond repair. (Bundesarchiv, Bild 101I-MW-1913-31, Schnellboot übernimmt Torpedos. jpg / Wikimedia Commons)

merchant shipping in the North Atlantic before damage forced *Scharnhorst* back to Wilhelmshaven. In May 1941 *Scharnhorst* left Brest in France, and fought in the 'Channel Dash' 11–13 Feb 1942 before sheltering in Gotenhafen. In Mar 1943 it sailed to Norway, taking part in the 'Spitsbergen Raid' in Sept, but was sunk by an RN squadron in the Battle of the North Cape on 26 Dec 1943. During Oct 1939 the *Gneisenau* attacked shipping in the North Sea and in Nov 1939 RN ships in the South Atlantic. After fighting in the

Norwegian campaign Apr–June 1940, it reached the Atlantic in Jan 1941, and took part in the Channel Dash in Feb 1942, but was retired from service in Apr 1942 and scuttled in May 1945.

Pocket battleships (*Panzerschiffe*) x 3

Unique to the German Navy, these capital ships were 'super-heavy cruisers' rather than true battleships. The Deutschland Class comprised *Deutschland / Lützow*, *Admiral Scheer* and *Admiral Graf Spee*. The *Deutschland* served in the North Atlantic from Sept 1939, then the Baltic from Jan 1940, being renamed *Lützow* in Feb 1940. The *Lützow* fought off Norway from 9 Apr 1940, but after being damaged by an RN submarine it remained in Germany until June 1941, when it was again torpedoed, by RAF aircraft while en route to the Atlantic. In Dec 1942 it returned to Norway, fighting in the 'battle of the Barents Sea' on 31 Dec, before returning to Germany in Sept 1943. After service as a training ship it helped to evacuate refugees from East Germany early in 1945, but was bombed on 16 Apr and scuttled on 4 May.

Admiral Scheer attacked merchant shipping in the Atlantic in Oct 1940 and in the South Atlantic in Dec, reaching Norway in Mar 1941 and the Arctic in Nov 1942. In 1945 it transported East German refugees before being bombed on 9 April.

Admiral Graf Spee left Wilhelmshaven in Aug 1939 and attacked merchant shipping in the South Atlantic until trapped in Montevideo, Uruguay by British cruisers at the Battle of the River Plate on 13 Dec 1939, and was scuttled on 17 Dec.

Aircraft carrier (*Flugzeugträger*) x 1

Changing priorities led to *Graf Zeppelin*, Germany's only aircraft carrier, being launched incomplete on 8 Dec 1938; work stopped in May 1940, and it was scuttled in Mar 1945 near Stettin (now Szczecin), Poland.

CRUISERS

Heavy cruisers (*Schwere Kreuzer*) x 5

The Hipper Class comprised *Admiral Hipper* and *Blücher*. In Feb 1940 *Admiral Hipper* joined *Gneisenau* and *Scharnhorst* in the North Sea before

Off Lorient, summer 1941: presumably photographed while surfaced to charge the batteries by running the diesel engine, crewmen of U-109 (*KK* Hans-Georg Fischer) enjoy sunshine and fresh air outside the oppressive confines of their boat – although the conning-tower watch keep a constant look-out. The men wear a casual variety of clothing; note (foreground) an M1941 tropical khaki on-board cap worn with a white shirt, dark shorts and canvas shoes. U-109 was a Type IXB boat, commissioned on 5 Dec 1940 and serving with *2. U-Flottille*. Later commanded by *Olt z S* Joachim Schramm, it would be sunk with all hands by Allied aircraft on 4 May 1943, during the war's worst month for the Atlantic 'wolf packs'. (Bundesarchiv, Bild 101II-MW-4287-16A / Wikimedia Commons)

fighting off Norway from 9 Apr 1940. It returned to Wilhelmshaven that autumn, finally reaching Brest, France, in Jan 1941, then docked in Germany in April. In Mar 1942 *Admiral Hipper* transferred to Trondheim, Norway, before returning to Germany, and was decommissioned on 1 Apr 1943. After transporting East German refugees, it was scuttled on 3 May 1945. The *Blücher* took part in the invasion of Norway on 9 Apr 1940, but was sunk that day by Norwegian coastal artillery.

The *Prinz Eugen* Class comprised *Prinz Eugen*, *Seydlitz* and *Lützow*. *Prinz Eugen* left Gotenhafen 18 May 1941 and fought with *Bismarck* in the North Atlantic, helping to sink HMS *Hood* before withdrawing to Brest for repairs. It fought in the Channel Dash 11–13 Feb 1942, but was later torpedoed by an RN submarine at Trondheim, Norway. It saw action against Soviet forces in June 1944, but after colliding with the light cruiser *Leipzig* on 15 Oct 1944 it was docked in Copenhagen until May 1945.

The *Seydlitz* was launched incomplete in Jan 1939, and scuttled in Königsberg on 10 Apr 1945. The *Lützow* was launched on 1 July 1939 and was sold to the Soviet Union on 11 Feb 1940, allowing the name to be transferred to the *Deutschland* (see above).

Light cruisers (*Leichte Kreuzer*) x 6

The *Emden* fought in the 1940 Norwegian campaign before becoming a training ship; during Operation 'Hannibal' it transported refugees to Kiel, where it was scuttled in May 1945.

The K Class comprised *Königsberg*, *Karlsruhe* and *Köln*. During the Norwegian campaign *Königsberg* was sunk on 10 Apr 1940 by RN dive-bombers, and was scrapped in 1943. In the same battle *Karlsruhe* was torpedoed by an RN submarine on 9 Apr and finished off by the German torpedo-boat *Greif*. *Köln* also fought in Norwegian waters Apr–June 1940, and in the invasion of the USSR in June 1941, before returning to Narvik in Aug 1942, and to the Baltic in 1943. In Oct 1944 it operated in Danish and Norwegian waters, being bombed in Dec 1944 and early 1945 while firing on Red Army troops, and finally sinking on 5 Apr 1945.

Leipzig was torpedoed in Dec 1939 by the British submarine HMS *Salmon*, and was subsequently converted to a training ship in Gotenhafen. On 15 Oct 1944 it collided with the *Prinz Eugen* and was disabled; surviving

---

TABLE 2: Selective battle order of submarines, 1 Sept 1935–8 May 1945

Front-Line Submarine Flotillas
(1). 'Weddingen' Flotilla (Sept 1935–Sept 1944): 111 boats (U8–U1199 series, UB, UD1, UD4). **(2). 'Salzwedel' Flotilla** (Sept 1936–Aug 1944): 91 boats (U25–U1228 series, UA, UD3). **(3). 'Lohs' Flotilla** (Oct 1937–Oct 1944): 108 boats (U10–U993 series, UB, UD1, UD3, UD4). **(5). 'Emsmann' Flotilla** (Dec 1938–Jan 1940): 7 boats (U56–U62 series); **became Training Flot. (6). Flotilla 'Hundius'** (Oct 1938–Aug 1944): 91 boats (U37–U999 series). **(7). 'Wegener' Flotilla** (June 1938–May 1945): 110 boats (U45–U1192 series, UA)
9. Flotilla (Oct 1941–Sept 1944): 84 boats (U89–U1165 series). **10. Flotilla** (Jan 1942–Aug 1944): 82 boats (U118–U1230 series, IXC/140). **11. Flotilla** (May 1942–May 1945): 189 boats (U88–U3008 series). **12. Flotilla** (Oct 1942–Aug 1944): 47 boats (U117–U1062 series; UIT21–25). **13. Flotilla** (June 1943–May 1945): 55 boats (U212–U1163 series). **14. Flotilla** (Dec 1944–May 1945): 8 boats (U294–U997 series). **23. Flotilla** (Sept 1941–May 1942): 9 boats (U75–U559 series). **29. Flotilla** (Dec 1941–Sept 1944): 52 boats (U29–U223 series). **30. Flotilla** (Oct 1942–Sept 1944): 6 boats (U9–U24 series). **33. Flotilla** (Sept 1944–May 1945): 76 boats (U155–U1305, UIT24–25)
Submarine Training Flotillas
4. Flotilla (May 1941–May 1945): 279 boats (U37–U3791 series). **5. Flotilla** (June 1941–May 1945): 353 boats (U11–U4712 series; UD1, UD3, UD4, UF2). **8. Flotilla** (Oct 1941–Feb 1945): 258 boats (U88–U2339 series). **18. Flotilla** (Jan–Mar 1945): 5 boats (U1008–U 1162 series; UA, UD4). **19. Flotilla** (Oct 1943–May 1945): 4 boats (U56–59). **20. Flotilla** (June 1943–Feb 1945), no assigned boats. **21. Flotilla** (1935–Mar 1945): provided boats for 1. Training Div. **22. Flotilla** (Jan 1941–May 1945): provided 47 boats (U8–U1198 series) for 2. Training Div. **23. Flotilla** (Sept 1943–Mar 1945 as Training Flot: 11 boats (U29–U978 series). **24. (1. Training) Flotilla** (Oct 1939–Mar 1945): 53 boats (U8–U1207 series; UA, UD4). **25. (2. Training) Flotilla** (May 1940–May 1945): supervised other boats' torpedo practice. **26. Flotilla** (Apr 1941–May 1945): 7 boats (U37–U351 series). **27. Flotilla** (Jan 1940–Apr 1945): 1 boat (UD-4). **29. Flotilla** (Dec 1941–Sept 1944): 52 boats (U73–U969 series). **30. Flotilla** (Oct 1942–Oct 1944): 6 boats (U9–U24 series). **31. Flotilla** (Sept 1943 – May 1945): 170 boats (U120–U2552 series). **32. Flotilla** (Aug 1944–May 1945): 43 boats (U2321–U3002 series)

Note: 'series' = 'Included boats with randomly assigned, non-sequential numbers between these two numbers'.

as a stationary gun-platform, it was scuttled post-war. *Nürnberg* was also torpedoed in Dec 1939 by HMS *Salmon* and was out of action until the next summer, when it returned to Germany via the Arctic in Aug 1940. It returned to Norway in Nov 1942, but was in Wilhelmshaven in May 1945, when it was transferred to the Soviet Navy as the *Admiral Makarov*.

Destroyers (*Zerstörer*) x 42

These ships were built in six classes, numbered Z1–Z36 and Z43–Z45, plus three captured (French, ZF2; Greek, ZG3; and Dutch, ZH1). Those numbered Z1–Z22 also received names, usually of German naval personnel who had distinguished themselves in World War I. The destroyers were grouped into seven flotillas, numbered 1–6 and 8, with 6–12 ships per flotilla (see Table 1, page 18). The classes were as below:

M1934 Destroyers (commissioned from 1937): 4 ships (Z1–Z4). **M1934A (Nov 1934–Jan 1935)**: 12 ships (Z5–Z16). **M1936 (1938–39)**: 6 ships (Z17–Z22). **M1936A (Sept 1940–Nov 1941)**: 8 ships (Z23–Z30). **M1936A (Mob) (Apr 1942–Aug 1944)**: 7 ships (Z31–Z39).[2] **M1936B (1942–44)**: 5 ships (Z35 & Z36, Z43–Z45).

Auxiliary cruisers (*Hilfskreuzer*) x 11

Auxiliary cruisers, known to the Allies as 'raiders', were German merchant ships armed and converted to attack enemy merchant shipping away from the main theatres of war. There were 11 auxiliary cruisers, all given random names and 10 assigned 'HSK' numbers 1–9, with *Hansa* numbered HSK5 (II) and *Coronel* lacking a number. Apart from in the North Sea these ships usually operated far from Germany, typically in the South Atlantic, Indian Ocean and South Pacific. Being lightly armed they usually avoided RN warships, often disguising themselves as Allied or neutral vessels. It is estimated that the auxiliary cruisers sank or captured about 140 Allied ships;

2 'Mob' = *Mobilisiert*, 'mobilised'; indicating improved class introduced in wartime.

C

MEDITERRANEAN, 1942

(C1) *Oberbootsmannsmaat*; Northern Mediterranean
This senior leading seaman wears the navy-blue on-board cap (*Bordmütze*), introduced on 7 Oct 1939 as a more practical replacement for the peakless sailors' cap (and sometimes the peaked cap) for shipboard duty. All ranks wore the eagle and cockade insignia. In cool weather, he wears over his jumper the thigh-length, double-breasted *Uberzieher* pea-jacket (nicknamed the '*Collani*', after a well-known maker) for junior NCOs and ratings, with a yellow breast eagle; the cornflower-blue collar patches (here with two gold rank braids) and the NCOs' gold-braid collar-edging were introduced on 1 Dec 1939. On his left sleeve are the yellow Line-branch NCOs' fouled anchor with a seniority chevron, above a torpedo-divers' red trade badge showing a diver's helmet and a one chevron.

(C2) *Korvettenkapitän* (*W*); North Africa, August 1942
This junior-grade commander's 'W' suffix indicates a weapon systems specialist, and he wears the Navy officers' brown tropical uniform introduced on 2 Dec 1941. The peaked cap with a plain brown cloth peak shows a gold-wire eagle,

oakleaf wreath, and (unlike the navy-blue cap) chin cords. The service tunic has a gold-wire breast eagle on brown backing. The plaited silver-cord shoulder straps on navy-blue underlay bear the gold-metal crossed-cannons branch badge of Artillery Engineers. He displays the Iron Cross in both classes, and wears the *Wehrmacht* officers' brown leather service belt with a brass two-claw buckle, but not its cross-brace.

(C3) *Funkmaat*; North Africa, October 1942
This highly decorated leading seaman radar operator is wearing the M1941 brown tropical uniform, generally resembling the Army's greener olive-brown version. The peaked tropical field cap and four-pocket service tunic both display the yellow machine-woven eagle on brown backing. The shoulder straps show only blue NCOs' edging; the Radar branch badge of an anchor and two lightning bolts has been removed for security in case of capture. Like C2's, the tunic lacks collar patches. On his right forearm he wears the *Wehrmacht* M1941 'AFRIKAKORPS' cuff title. The tropical belt is brown webbing with a yellow-metal buckle plate, but the pistol holster is of dark brown leather.

the highest scorer was *Pinguin* with 33 'hits', the lowest being *Stier* with four, and *Hansa* and *Coronel* with none. The raiders were sometimes diverted to other duties, such as refuelling submarines, and *Hansa* helped transport Baltic refugees in Apr 1945.

TABLE 3: Selective battle order of anti-mine, dedicated anti-submarine, patrol & security vessels, 1 Sept 1939–8 May 1945

42 Minesweeper Flotillas

1. Flotilla: M1, M3–M5, M7, M8, M14, M15, M17, M18, M20, M36, M37, M132, M155, M203, M204, M255, M256 (1934–June 1946). **2. Flotilla:** M2, M6, M9, M10–M13, M21, M25, M38, M152, M156 (1936–June 1944); M606–608, M611, M805, M806 (Feb 1945–Nov 1947). **3. Flotilla:** M15–19, M22, M29, M30, M151. **4. Flotilla:** M61, M89, M136, M510, M511, M534, M582, M584 (Sept 1930–Mar 1945); M1, M2, M81, M101, M132, M151, M203, M204, M255 (Apr–May 1945). **5. Flotilla:** M4, M23, M31, M35, M81, M154, M201, M202, M205, M251–M253 (Dec 1940–Oct 1947). **6. Flotilla:** M4, M23, M31, M35, M81, M154, M201, M202, M205, M251–M253 (Sept 1939–Jan 1942); M38, M39, M82–M85, M102, M133, M155, M156, M206, M256, M265, M267 (May 1942–Aug 1944).**7. Flotilla:** M75, M84, M85, M102, M122, M126 (Sept 1939–Mar 1940); M39, M82, M83, M102, M153–M156, M205, M206 (Jan–May 1942); M23, M32, M33, M82, M102–104, M131, M201, F4–5, F7. **8. Flotilla:** M24, M26–M28, M32, M34, M152, M254, M256, M265, M277, M292, M329, M370 (early 1941–May 1945). **9. Flotilla:** M272–M274, M276, M306, M326, M346, M348, M364, M365 (Mar 1943–June 1947). **10. Flotilla:** M263, M264, M275, M307, M347, M366, M367, M385, M408, M428, M439 (Apr 1943–Sept 1944). **11. Flotilla:** 12 fishing-boats (Sept 1939–Aug 1942); M264, M291, M307, M327, M347, M348, M368, M386 (Aug 1943–Feb 1945).**12. Flotilla:** M601–M605, M612, M801–M804 (Sept 1939–Oct 1942; Nov 1944–Nov 1947).

13. Flotilla (Sept 1939–Dec 1942). **14. Flotilla** (Sept 1939–Aug 1941). **15. Flotilla** (Sept 1939–Mar 1943). **16. Flotilla** (Oct 1939–Jan 1943). **17. Flotilla** (Sept 1939–Nov 1942). **18. Flotilla** (Sept 1939–Nov 1942). **19. Flotilla** (Sept 1939–Oct 1943).

21. Flotilla: M82, M103, M261, M305, M323, M324, M327, M341–M343, M362, M383, M504, M526, M545 (Jan 1942–Apr 1945). **22. Flotilla:** M301–03, M321, M322, M361, M368, M381, M382, M436 (Sept 1941–Jan 1948). **23. Flotilla:** M324, M401, M411, M421, M423, M431, M441, M443, M467, M468 (Oct 1942–1947). **24. Flotilla:** M343, M402, M412, M422, M432, M438, M442, M452, M475 (Nov 1942–May 1945). **25. Flotilla:** M278, M294, M295, M328, M330, M341, M342, M403, M413, M423, M433, M451, M453, M459, M460 (Dec 1942–Nov 1947). **26. Flotilla:** M404, M424, M434, M444, M454, M476, M486, M495 (Jan 1943–Aug 1944). **27. Flotilla:** M261, M323, M327, M329, M362, M369, M405, M414, M425, M434, M345, M461, M469, M471, M484 (Jan 1943–Aug 1944) **28. Flotilla:** M262, M271, M304, M325, M344, M345, M363, M384, M463 (Dec 1942–Aug 1944). **29. Flotilla:** M265, M267, M293, M301, M386, M403, M415, M426, M436, M445, M455, M462, M470 (Oct 1943–June 1946). **30. Flotilla:** M266, M291, M348, M407, M416, M427, M437, M446, M456, M469, M489 (Mar 1943–June 1945).

31. Flotilla (Sept 1940–Dec 1947). **32. Flotilla** (June 1940–Jun 1945). **34. Flotilla** (June 1940–May 1945). **36. Flotilla** (July 1940–May 1945), **38. Flotilla** (July 1940–May 1945). **40. Flotilla** (July 1940–Sept 1944). **42. Flotilla** (July 1940–Sept 1944). **44. Flotilla** (Nov 1940–Sept 1944). **46. Flotilla** (Dec 1941–May 1945). **52. Flotilla:** M1, M2, M534 (Dec 1940–Oct 1944). **54. Flotilla** (Jan 1941–1944). **56. Flotilla** (June 1940–May 1945). **70. Flotilla** (July 1943–Oct 1944).

20 Clearance Minesweeper Flotillas

1. Flotilla (–1948); **2. Flotilla** (–1945); **3. Flotilla** (–1944); **4. Flotilla** (1939 –45); **5. Flotilla** (Aug 1939–Dec 1945); **6. Flotilla** (1941–45); **7. Flotilla** (Oct 1940–Nov 1946); **8. Flotilla** (1942–47); **9. Flotilla** (1942–47); **10. Flotilla** (Mar 1942–Aug 1944); **11. Flotilla** (1939–Oct 1940); **12. Flotilla** (May 1942–1945); **13. Flotilla** (1943–57); **14. Flotilla** (1943–46); **15. Flotilla** (1945); **16. Flotilla** (Oct 1944–Dec 1947); **17. Flotilla** (July 1944–Dec 1947); **21. Flotilla** (1943–Dec 1945); **25. Flotilla** (1945); **30. Flotilla** (1943).

7 Auxiliary Minesweeper Flotillas

1. Flotilla (Sept 1939–1946); **2. Flotilla** (1939–44); **3. Flotilla** (1940–46); **4. Flotilla** (1940–43); **5. Flotilla** (became **8. Flotilla**, 1941); **6. Flotilla** (July–Sept 1941).

31 Patrol Boat Flotillas

1. Flotilla (Oct 1939–Oct 1940); **2. Flotilla** (Sept 1939–Dec 1944); **3. Flotilla** (Sept 1939–May 1945); **4. Flotilla** (Sept 1939–Sept 1944); **6. Flotilla** (1944–45); **7. Flotilla** (Sept 1939–Sep 1944); **8. Flotilla** (Sept 1939–May 1945); **9. Flotilla** (Sept 1939–May 1945); **10. Flotilla** (Sept 1939; Oct 1943 **became 10. Security Flot.**); **11. Flotilla** (Sept 1939–May 1945); **12. Flotilla** (Oct 1939–Dec 1947); **13. Flotilla** (Sept 1939–Jan 1945); **14. Flotilla** (Feb 1943–May 1945); **15. Flotilla** (Sept 1939–May 1945); **16. Flotilla** (Oct 1940–May 1945); **17. Flotilla** (July 1940–May 1945); **18. Flotilla** (Oct 1940– May 1945); **19. Flotilla** (July 1940; Oct 1943 **became 5 Security Flot.**); **20. Flotilla** (July 1940–May 1945); **51. Flotilla** (1941–May 1945); **53. Flotilla** (1941–June 1945); **55. Flotilla** (1941–June 1945); **57. Flotilla** (Nov 1940–June 1945); **59. Flotilla** (Jan 1941–May 1945); **61. Flotilla** (Nov 1940–May 1946); **63. Flotilla** (May 1944–June 1945); **64. Flotilla** (June 1944–June 1945); **65. Flotilla** (May 1944–June 1945); **66. Flotilla** (May 1944–June 1945); **67. Flotilla** (July 1944–June 1945); **68. Flotilla** (May 1944–June 1945).

16 Security Flotillas

1., 2., 3. & 4. Security Flotillas (Oct 1943–May 1945); **5. Security Flotilla** (Oct 1943–June 1945); **6. Security Flotilla** (Jan 1943–June 1945); **7., 8., 9. & 10. Security Flotillas** (Oct 1943–May 1945); **11. Security Flotilla** (May 1943–Jan 1944); **12. Security Flotilla** (Oct 1943–June 1945); **13. Security Flotilla** (1944–45); **14. Security Flotilla** (1944–May 1945); **15. Security Flotilla** (Aug 1943–June 1945); **16. Security Flotilla** (Jan 1944–May 1945).

10 Submarine Hunter Flotillas

1. UJ Flotilla: 18 vessels (June 1943–Aug 1944). **2. UJ Flotilla:** 11 vessels (Mar–Dec 1944). **3. UJ Flotilla:** 19 vessels (Jan–Aug 1944). **11. UJ Flotilla:** 24 vessels (Sept 1939–June 1945). **12. UJ Flotilla** (Sept 1939–1941). **13. UJ Flotilla:** 45 vessels (1941–May 1945). **14. UJ Flotilla:** 35 vessels (1941–May 1945). **17. UJ Flotilla:** 57 vessels (July 1939–May 1945). **21 UJ Flotilla** (1942–44). **22. UJ Flotilla** (Dec 1942–Apr 1945); **23. UJ Flotilla** (May 1944–June 1945).

33 Patrol Boat Flotillas

1. Flotilla (Sept 1939); **2., 3., 4. & 5. Flotillas** (1944); **6. Flotilla** (1942–45); **8. Flotilla** (Oct 1943); **9. & 10. Flotillas** (Oct 1943); **11. Flotilla** (1943–44); **12. Flotilla** (1944–May 1945); **13., 14., 15. & 16. Flotillas** (1944).

7 Escort Boat Flotillas

1. & 2. Flotillas (1944); **3. Flotilla** (1942); **4. Flotilla** (1943); **5. Flotilla** (1944); **30. Flotilla** (1943–44); **31. Flotilla**.

Torpedo boats (*Torpedoboote*) x 109

Larger and armed for more diverse roles than British MTBs & MGBs, these small warships were ordered in eight classes. The first 14 boats were named after birds of prey (*Raubvogel*) or predators (*Raubtier*); the next 21 were numbered T1–T21. These M1923–M1937 classes all displaced about 600 tons. From 1939, 36 fleet torpedo boats (*Flottentorpedoboote*) were ordered, numbered T22–T72, but only T22–T36 were completed. Displacing 1,754 tons and mounting 4x 10.5cm guns and 6x torpedo-tubes, these fleet boats had capabilities comparable to destroyer escorts.

On paper, the classes ordered were as follows, but note: none of the M1941 fleet class was completed; the M1944 fleet class was cancelled; and of the 12x 2,566-ton M1940 fleet class ordered from captured Dutch yards, armed with 4x 5-in. guns and 8x torpedo tubes, only 3 were launched, uncompleted.

M1923 **Torpedo boats (1926)**: 6 boats named *Albatros*, *Falke*, *Greif*, *Kondor*, *Möwe*, *Seeadler*. **M1924 (1927–28)**: 8 boats named *Iltis*, *Jaguar*, *Leopard*, *Luchs*, *Löwe*, *Panther*, *Tiger*, *Wolf*. **M1935 (1939–40)**: 12 boats numbered T1–T12. **M1937 (1941)**: 9 boats numbered T13–T21.

M1939 Fleet torpedo boats (1939): 15 boats numbered T22–T36. **M1940 (1940)**: 12 boats numbered T61–T72 (only 3 launched, uncompleted). **M1941**: 15 boats numbered T37–T51 (none completed). **M1944**: 9 boats numbered T52–T60 (cancelled).

Additionally, the Navy was supposed to receive 46 commandeered foreign torpedo boats (of which 38 were commissioned), allotting them 'TA' numbers (for *Torpedoboote Ausland*): **June 1940**: 6 French Navy (TA1–TA6), not commissioned due to sabotage and bomb damage; 2 Norwegian Navy (TA7 & 7A8), not completed. **Apr 1941**: 2 Yugoslav Navy (TA48 & TA49). **Apr 1943**: 31 Royal Italian Navy (TA9–TA13, TA16–TA30, TA35–TA42, TA45–TA47).

The 109 German and serviceable foreign torpedo boats were allotted to nine flotillas (numbered 1.–7., 9. & 10.) with approximately four boats per flotilla. Note that 22 of the Italian boats were allotted to the 9th and 10th Flotillas.

Speed boats (*Schnellboote*) x 170

These smaller, faster craft, displacing about 92 tons, were collectively known to the Allies by the imprecise term 'E-boats' (for 'Enemy boats'). The *S-Boote* mounted 2 torpedo tubes; either a 37mm, 40mm, or single or quad-20mm stern gun; 1 single and one twin 20mm, plus machine-guns. Operating in the English Channel, Atlantic Ocean, Baltic, Mediterranean and Black Seas, they claimed approximately 140 Allied vessels sunk, including 101 merchant ships, two British destroyers and 11 British minesweepers. A total of 148 *S-Boote* were built in 11 classes, of which 122 boats saw operational service, in addition to some of 48 captured boats. They were allotted to 14 flotillas, numbered 1.–11., 21., 22. & 24.; in July 1943 five flotillas (3., 7., 21., 22. & 24.) formed the 1st S-Boat Division. The classes were as follows:

M1930 Class: one boat numbered S1. **S2 Class (1932)**: four boats numbered S2–S5. **S6 Class (1933–34)**: four boats numbered S6–S9. **S10 Class (1935)**: four boats numbered S10–S13. **S14 Class (1938)**: four boats numbered S14–S17. **S18 Class (1939)**: eight boats numbered S18–S25. **S26 Class (1940)**: four boats numbered S26–S29. **S30 Class (1941)**: 16 boats numbered S30–S37 & S54–S61. **S38 Class (1943)**: 16 boats numbered S38–S53, S62–S99, S101–S135, S137 & S138 (S159–S166 not completed). **S100 Class (1943)**:

78 boats numbered S100, S136, S139–S150, S167–S228 & S242–S243. **S701 Class (1945):** 9 boats numbered S701–S709.

Captured: 2 British (RA9, RA10); 10 Dutch (S151–S158, S201 & S202); 4 Yugoslav (S1–S5); 31 Italian (S501–S512, S601–S603, S621–S629, SA1–SA7); 1 Bulgarian (also S1).

ANTI-MINE, ANTI-SUBMARINE, PATROL & SECURITY VESSELS

Minesweepers (*Minensuchboote*) x 254

These *M-Boote* were used for minesweeping, minelaying, escort duties and anti-submarine warfare. Three classes were built, totalling 254 minesweepers numbered M1–M813;

Class M1935/39 (Mob) (1937): 69 ships numbered M1–M39, M81–M85, M101–M104, M131–M133, M151–M156, M201–M206 & M251–M256.

Class M1940 (1941): 106 ships numbered M261–M267, M271–M279, M291–M294, M301– M308, M321–M330, M341, M348, M361–M378, M381–M389, M401–M408, M411–M416, M421–M428, M431–M438, M441–M446, M452–M456, M459–M463, M467–M471, M475–M476, M483, M484, M486, M489, M495 & M496.

Class M1943 (1943): 79 ships numbered M601–M666 & M801–M813.

At least 235 minesweepers served in flotillas (see Table 3, page 24), usually with 10–15 boats per flotilla, and were supplemented by about 68 converted German, French, Dutch and Norwegian fishing-boats. There were 42 active minesweeping flotillas, numbered 1.–19., 21.–32., 34., 36., 38., 40., 43., 44., 46., 52., 54., 56. & 70.

Clearance minesweepers (*Räumboote*) x 349

R-Boote were smaller minesweepers, usually of wooden construction,

THE U-BOAT WAR

(D1) *Kapitänleutnant*; Atlantic, 1942
Full beards were authorized for all ranks of U-boat crews while at sea, due to the shortage of fresh water; senior ranks also had great latitude in their choice of clothing, including civilian sweaters and shirts. This lieutenant-commander wears the boat commander's traditional white cover on his peaked cap. An oversized crown was popular with junior officers and senior NCOs, and its peak has the junior officers' 'wavy' line of gold-wire edging. Just visible on his left side of the band is an unofficial metal flotilla badge, as sometimes painted on boat conning towers – in this case, the 'shark-finned sawfish' of 9. *U-Flottille*. The navy-blue service dress tunic shows the Line star above the medium/ narrow/ medium cuff rings of this rank. The yellow-metal Submarine War Badge is displayed below his Iron Cross 1st Class.

(D2) *Oberwaffenwart*; France, 1944
This Artillery Machinist ashore has reached the Navy's most senior warrant officer rank. He wears the navy-blue peaked cap with a plain peak, and, for working, the brown barracks service dress, with a gold-wire breast eagle. His navy-blue shoulder straps, edged in yellow NCO braid, show the unique combination of three 4-point silver stars and a gold metal chevron for *Oberwaffenwart*, with the branch badge of a crossed unfouled anchor and cannon. Evidence of his previous service at sea, presumably in a deck-gun team, are the Submarine War Badge and Iron Cross 1st Class.

(D3) U-Boat crewman; American waters, 1942
This rating, again with a 'deep sea' beard, wears the single-breasted, standing-collar version of the submarine crewmen's grey leather protective clothing. This was worn by all engineering personnel, diesel and electrical mechanics, and helmsmen. 'Deck' personnel (the watch officers, coxswain/ navigator, gunnery personnel, torpedo mechanics and also radio operators and signallers) received a longer thigh-length double-breasted jacket, with a wide, lapelled collar; deep shoulder-yoke reinforcement; vertical 'hand-warmer' pockets above the flapped hip pockets; and a rear half-belt. It was occasionally seen with NCOs' white-metal 'chevrons', in imitation of uniform collar braid, attached to the collar points. Other protective gear carried on U-boats were black oilskin two-piece suits with matching 'balaclavas' and sou'wester hats, and navy-blue knitted '*Pudelmützen*' bobble caps. This rating's on-board cap sports the unofficial 'red devil' badge of U-552 (*KL* Erich Topp), a Type VIIC boat of 7. *U-Flottille*, which sank seven ships totalling nearly 46,000 tons during one patrol off the American east coast in Mar–Apr 1942, during the 'Second Happy Time'.

Kapitänleutnant Erich Topp (right), commander of U-552, and behind him *Lt z S* Schwich, his IWO ('first watch officer', i.e. first lieutenant or executive officer), returning to the *7. U-Flottille* base at St Nazaire after his second patrol in 1941. Topp would survive the war as the third-ranking U-boat ace, having sunk 35 ships during 13 patrols. Awarded the Swords to his Knight's Cross with Oakleaves (11 Apr 1941), and the U-Boat War Badge with Diamonds (11 Apr 1942), Topp later commanded the 27th Submarine (Training) Flotilla. Here he wears British Army denim fatigues, with added gold buttons, shoulder straps of rank, and a white cord lanyard to the left pocket. Captured in large numbers from the British Expeditionary Force in France in summer 1940, the denims were a serviceable substitute for the German Navy's grey-green fatigues. (Bundesarchiv, Bild 101II-MW-3676-28 / Buchheim, Lothar-Günther / CC-BY-SA 3.0 Wikimedia Commons)

employed in coastal waters and harbours. Nine classes were built, totalling 349 ships numbered between R1 and R448:

Class R1 (1929): 16 ships numbered R1–R16. **Class R17 (1934)**: 8 ships numbered R17–R24. **Class R25 (1938)**: 16 ships numbered R25–R40. **Class R41 (1939)**: 89 ships numbered R41–R129. **Class R130 (1943)**: 21 ships numbered R130–R150. **Class R151 (1940)**: 67 ships numbered R151–R217. **Class R218 (M1943)**: 72 ships numbered R218–270 & R272–R290. **Class R301 (1942)**: 12 ships numbered R301–R312. **Class R401 (1942)**: 48 ships numbered R401–R448.

There were also 73 captured enemy minesweepers, allocated RA numbers: 8 French (RA1–RA8); 2 British (RA9 & RA10); 6 Dutch (RA51–RA56); and 57 Italian (RA251–RA268, RA RD101–RD101, RA105). *R–Boote* were allocated to 20 flotillas, numbered 1.–17., 21., 25. & 30., operating in the North Sea, Baltic Sea, Black Sea, and on the coasts of Norway, Denmark, Belgium, the Netherlands and Russia, between Oct 1940 and early 1948 (see above, 'German Minesweeping Administration 1945–48').

Auxiliary minesweepers (*Sperrbrecher*)

Sperrbrecher (literally 'barricade breakers') were minesweepers which spearheaded flotillas entering minefields to detonate mines with their reinforced hulls – a dangerous manoeuvre which inevitably caused heavy losses. Some vessels were armed with AA guns. They were organized into six flotillas, numbered 1.–4., 5. (later renumbered 8.) and 6.

Patrol & Security Boats (*Vorpostenboote & Sicherungsboote*)

Coastal patrol boats were numbered with 'V' or 'VP' prefixes and allocated to 31 flotillas, numbered 1.–4., 6.–20., 51., 53., 55., 57., 59., 61., & 63.–68.

Security boats were small launches used for harbour patrol and other in-shore duties. From 1943 they were divided into 16 security flotillas numbered 1.–16.

Submarine-hunters (*Unterseebootsjäger*)

About 300 German, French, Italian and Norwegian fishing-boats, cutters and whaling boats were commandeered by the German Navy as submarine-hunters. These were organized into ten *U-Bootjagdflottillen* numbered 1.–3., 11., 12., 13 (later14.), 17., & 21.–23. Each boat was numbered UJ + 1 or 2 sequential flotilla numerals + 1 to 3 sequential boat numerals (e.g. 'UJ1109' was the ninth boat of the 11th Flotilla).

Escort boats (*Geleitboote*)

Escort vessels were tasked with protecting other naval and merchant ships from sea and air attack. Plans to construct dedicated classes of escort ships were abandoned in Nov 1942, and from Mar 1943 various vessels were simply designated for this task. They were organized into 7 *Geleitflottillen* numbered 1.–5., 30. & 31. German ships were numbered F + sequential numbers, non-German ships TA + sequential numbers.

SUBMARINES

Unterseeboote x *c*.1,400

The *U-Boote* formed the largest and, during the first 40 months of the war, the most successful arm of the German Navy. Within eight main Roman-numbered types, some 19 sub-types were identifiable. Boats were individually numbered, but the sequence was often incomplete, particularly above U1010. Omitting here boats ordered but later cancelled, damaged or destroyed by air

A *Neger* one-man torpedo-carrying submersible or 'human torpedo', as used by the *Lehrkommando 350* units of the *K-Verbände* special forces. A small plexiglass dome covers the pilot's protruding head, and ahead of this is the simple aiming-post used when discharging the lower torpedo. Of some 200 built, 30 were deployed at Anzio on 20 Apr 1944, sinking three ships and damaging harbour installations. Another 26 were deployed off Normandy during 5–7 July, sinking two destroyers and three minesweepers. In mid-August improved *Marten* versions of this craft sank a destroyer and an ammunition ship and damaged others, but German losses were always unacceptably high. (Neger human torpedo.jpg)

This Arado Ar196 reconnaissance floatplane rests on the catapult of the heavy cruiser *Admiral Hipper* during 1943. It belongs to the *Luftwaffe 1. Staffel, I/ 196 Bordfliegergruppe*, commanded by Maj Gerrit Wiegmink. The Arado Ar196 was the most successful German light floatplane built; *Admiral Hipper* carried three, and altogether the *Kriegsmarine* capital ships carried 35–40 during their deployments in the Atlantic, Baltic and Arctic. (Bundesarchiv, Bild 101II-MW-1949-03 / Hipper / CC-BY-SA 3.0? Wikimedia Commons)

raids during production or otherwise not completed, and those used only for experimental trials, those commissioned were as follows:

Type I (U25, U26). Type IIA (U1–U6). Type IIB (U7–U24, U120 & U121). Type IIC (U56–U63); Type IID (U137–U152).

Type VIIA (U27– U36). Type VIIB (U45–U55, U73–U76, U83–U87, U99–U102, & U1405–U1407). Type VIIC (U69–U72, U77–U82, U88–U98, U132–U136, U201–U212, U221–U232, U235–U291, U301– U329, U331–U394, U396–U458, U465–U486, U551–U683, U685–U699, U701–U722, U731–U779, U821–U822, U825–U840, U901–U908, U921–U930, U951–U1031, U1051–U1065, & U1063–U1079). Type VIIC/41 (U292–U300, U1101–U1220, & U1271–U1404). Type VIID (U213–U218). Type VIIF (U1059–U1062).

Type IXA (U37–U44). Type IXB (U64, U65, U103–U111, & U122–U124). Type IXC (U66–U68, U125–U131, U153–U166, U171–U176, & U501–U524). Type IXC/40 (U167–U170, U183–U194, U525–U550, U801–U806, U841–U846, U583–U589, U565–U859, U865–U859, U865–U870, U877–U881, U1221–U1262, & U1501–U1530). Type IXD-1 (U189, U195). Type IXD-2 (U177–U179, U181, U182, U196–U200, U847–U852, U859–U864, & U871–U876). Type IXD/42 (U883).

Type XB (U116–U119, U219, U220, U233 & U234). Type XIV (U459 –U464, & U487–U490). Type XXI (U2501–U2546, U2548–U2551, U3001– U3035, U3037–U3041, U3044, & U3501–U3530). Type XXIII (U2321–U2500, U4001– U4120, & U4701–U4891).

There were also 36 captured enemy submarines: 1 British (UB); 5 Dutch (UD1–UD5); 3 French (UF1–UF3). 2 Norwegian (UC1 & UC2); 24 Italian (UIT1–UIT16 & UIT18–UIT25); and 1 Turkish (UA).

The U-boats were allotted to numbered flotillas, usually comprising about ten boats at a time (see Table 2, page 21). However, the varying histories of the flotillas meant that, for example, the 11th Flotilla recorded a total of 189 boats in the three years of its existence, but the 12th only 48. There were 16 numbered front-line flotillas; the 1.–3. and 5.–7. *Flottillen* also bore the names of famous naval officers, scientists and towns, while the other ten flotillas (9.–14., 23., 29., 30. & 33.) had numbers only. The main Atlantic coast flotillas were 1. & 9. (at Brest), 2. & 10. (Lorient), 3. (La Rochelle), 6. & 7. (St Nazaire) and 12. (Bordeaux). There were also 17 training flotillas in home waters, numbered 4., 5., 8., 18.–23., 24(1)., 25(2)., 26., 27., & 29–32).

SPECIAL FORCES

Among others, numbers of U-boat veterans subsequently volunteered for the *Kleinkampfverbände* (*K-Verbände* – literally, 'small battle units') of combat swimmers and naval commandos. These operated between Apr 1944 and May 1945, with HQ at Heiligenhafen, commanded by *Konteradmiral* Hellmuth Heye; in Oct 1944 they numbered *c.*8,000 personnel of all categories.[3]

Development and training units were termed *Lehrkommandos* (sing. LKdo), each servicing up to ten operational *Kampf-Flottillen* (K-Flot). Flotillas from more than one LKdo might operate in concert, and/ or supported by *Schnellboote*. Many personnel were lost in training accidents or in action, particularly pilots of midget submersibles/ manned torpedoes. Early *Seehund* missions (Jan 1945), and all by the *Molch* (Sept 1944–Mar 1945), suffered 60–80 per cent losses from up to 18 craft deployed at a time, for negligible or no returns. Nevertheless, some survived to master the difficulties, and achieved a number of sinkings. The most successful elements were LKdo 300's *Seehund* crews from Feb 1945 onward, who claimed about 120,000 total tonnage sunk, and Lkdo 350's *Neger* and *Marder* manned torpedoes, which sank several Allied warships at Anzio and off Normandy. Units were as follows:

Lehrkommando 200 (Kampf-Flottillen 211–220) Priesterbeck, later Plön; operated *Linsen* speedboats packed with explosives for ramming ('*Sprengboote*').

LKdo 250 (K-Flot 261–270) Lübeck; operated *Biber* one-man submersibles.

LKdo 300 (K-Flot 311–316) Neustadt; operated *Hecht* two-man submersibles (training only), and *Seehund* two-man midget submarines.

LKdo 350 (K-Flot 361–366) Surendorf; operated *Neger* and *Marder* one-man piloted torpedoes.

LKdo 400 (K-Flot 411–417) Surendorf; operated *Molch* one-man submersibles.

LKdo 600 (K-Flot 611–615) Trained with assault boats for commando operations from Italian coasts. Re-organized into 4 independent assault boat flotillas: K-Flot 611 became *1. Sturmboot-Flottille* (Ligurian Sea, Aug 1944): K-Flot 612 became 2. S-Flot (Adriatic Sea, Nov 1944); K-Flot 613 IIa became 3. S-Flot; S-Flot 615 was re-formed (Mar 1945).

LKdo 700 (K-Flot 702 & 704) Trained combat frogmen/ commandos for clandestine raids, often against bridges, NW Europe & Eastern Front (June 1944–May 1945).

NAVAL AVIATION

Reichsmarschall Goering insisted that all German flight personnel should belong to the *Luftwaffe*; consequently, no separate naval air arm was formed. *Luftwaffe* aircraft attached to the Navy were organized in *Gruppen* (equivalent to RAF wings), each comprising 1 to 3 *Staffeln* (squadrons). Only the most important units are listed here:

3 See also Elite 177, *German Special Forces in World War II*.

Nine Coastal Air Wings (*Küstenfliegergruppen*), numbered 106, 206, 306, 406, 506, 606, 706, 806 and 906, were active on reconnaissance duties July 1936–Nov 1944. They flew Heinkel He 60, He 114 and He 115 floatplanes, Dornier Do 18 and Blohm und Voß 138 flying-boats, and Junkers Ju 88A bombers.

Three Reconnaissance Wings (Sea) (*Aufklärungsgruppen* (*See*)), numbered 125–127, were formed 1 Apr–1 Oct 1936. On 13 July 1943 they were redesignated Sea Reconnaissance Wings (*Seeaufklärungsgruppen*) and enhanced to a total of six wings numbered 126–131. Some units fought on until May 1945, operating Arado and Heinkel floatplanes and Blohm und Voß flying-boats.

Bordfliegergruppe I/ 196 (Shipborne Air Wing I/ 196) served Oct 1937–Apr 1945; it comprised *1. Staffel* (Oct 1937–Mar 1945) and *5. Staffel* (Oct 1937–mid-1943). Wing II/ 196 existed briefly in 1937, and subsequently its *2. Staffel* (8 Aug 1943–3 June 1944) and *3. Staffel* (Oct 1943–Mar 1944) served as independent squadrons. These four squadrons deployed He 60 and later Ar 196 floatplanes from aboard Germany's capital ships, launched from catapults and recovered by cranes. About 35–40 aircraft in total were carried on the four battleships and eight heavy cruisers: *Bismarck* & *Tirpitz*, 4–6 aircraft; *Scharnhorst* & *Gneisenau*, 3–4 aircraft; *Admiral Hipper*, *Blücher*, *Lützow*, *Seydliz* & *Prinz Eugen*, 3 aircraft; *Admiral Graf Spee*, *Admiral Scheer* & *Deutschland/ Lützow*, 2 aircraft.

NAVAL LAND FORCES

NAVAL INFANTRY

Three Naval Divisions had fought in World War I, composed of Naval Infantry (*Marineinfanterie*) – sailors equipped and fighting as infantry. In Mar 1938 1st Naval Assault Company (*1. Marine-Stoßtrupp-Kompanie* – MSK) was formed with two infantry platoons, a heavy-weapons platoon

ATLANTIC & BALTIC, 1943–45

(E1) *Großadmiral* **Karl Dönitz; Wilhelmshaven, spring 1943**

Konteradmiral Dönitz was appointed Commander of Submarines (*Führer der Unterseeboote*) on 17 Oct 1939, and on 31 Jan 1943 he was promoted to *Großadmiral* and Commander-in-Chief of the Navy (*Oberbefehlshaber der Kriegsmarine*). He is wearing the flag officers' navy-blue service dress with an M1935 greatcoat; note the white shirt worn without the black tie, to accommodate his Knight's Cross with Oakleaves, awarded on 6 Apr 1943. The admirals' greatcoat is immediately distinguishable by its cornflower-blue internal lapel facings, worn exposed, and its interwoven gold-and-silver cord shoulder straps. The distinctions of this 'Admiral of the Fleet' rank are crossed silver batons on the shoulder straps, and the navy-blue and gold personalized baton which he holds. The silver-braid M1935 ceremonial belt, with a gold clasp, supports a gold-furnished dress dagger with a silver knot. Obscured at this angle, the trousers have cornflower-blue seam piping between two stripes.

(E2) *Bootsmann*, **1st Mine Clearance Flotilla; Gulf of Finland, 1943**

This Spanish Navy senior petty officer has volunteered to serve on *Räumboote* in one of the four Spanish-manned flotillas which operated around Kotka on the southern coast of Finland. His service dress uniform bears the shoulder straps of this German rank and branch, with a single 4-point silver star, a gold fouled anchor and gold braid edging. The only Spanish feature is the red-and-yellow national flag shield-patch, with the yellow-on-black top title 'ESPAÑA', on his upper right sleeve.

(E3) *Gefreiter*, **7th Depot Battalion; Stralsund, January 1943**

This able seaman, whose unit is being absorbed into the *3. Schiffstammregiment*, is wearing the Navy's M1935 field-grey walking-out dress. All his 'anchor' buttons are now painted grey-green. His M1934 field cap has the same insignia as that in Plate B1. On the dark green collar, the patches have light grey *Litzen* with yellow centre-stripes (in British parlance, 'lights') and a white separation stripe, on dark green backing. The pointed M1940 field-grey shoulder straps have gold buttons and the Depot units' gold-metal crossed-anchors branch badge, but the gold Roman battalion numerals have been removed. He wears a yellow machine-woven rank chevron on a dark-green triangular backing on his left upper arm. For this order-of-dress his field-grey M1940 trousers hang loose over his boots.

and an engineer platoon, for local raids. It fought in the Spanish Civil War in 1938, and helped occupy Memel (now Klaipėda, Lithuania) on 25 Mar 1939. During 1–7 Sept 1939 the 230-strong company, under *Oberleutnant (MA)* Wilhelm Henningsen (k.i.a. 2 Sept, replaced by *Olt (MA)* Walter Schug) attacked the Polish Military Transit Depot at Westerplatte, Danzig. By June 1940 it had expanded to a 6-coy battalion (*Abteilung*), serving in Norway, at Cherbourg, France, and in the Channel Islands. In Dec 1941 the unit was redesignated 531st Naval Artillery Bn; it fought in Russia under Army Group North, at Leningrad and in the Oranienbaum Pocket (1943–44), Narva (now Saaremaa, Estonia) and Oesel, Finland (1944), and Gotenhafen and Hela (now Gdynia and Hel, Poland) in 1945.

During the war it became standard practice to form infantry units (usually named after their commanders) from Navy destroyer crews whose ships were out of action, beginning Apr–June 1940 with Berger Naval Rgt and Kothe, Erdmenger and Freytag Naval Bns. These were followed in Nov 1943 by Klüver Bn; in Jan 1944 by Hoßfeld and Klemm Bns; in Aug 1944 by Weber Bde in Bordeaux; and in Nov 1944 by *Nord* (North) Rifle Bde at Husum, northern Germany.

Early in 1945, as Allied forces pressed toward Germany's frontiers from both west and east, six Naval/ Naval Inf Divs (*Marine-Divisionen*, from 10 Mar 1945 *Marine-Infanterie-Divisionen*) were formed around Army cadres to join the defensive fighting. Each was to be organized as a Type 45 Inf Div, with three 2-bn Naval Grenadier (Inf) Rgts; a light Naval Fusilier Bn (bicycles); a Naval Arty Rgt and Naval AT Bn; a Naval Engineer Bn, Naval Signals Bn, Naval Field Replacement Bn and a Supply Rgt. These mostly understrength divisions in fact had few integral heavy weapons.

1st Naval Division was formed (31 Jan 1945) in Stettin (now Szczecin, Poland) from Rifle Bde *Nord*. Moved south, it fought, without much effect, to defend this sector of the Oder Front until May 1945.

2nd Naval Infantry Division was formed (31 Jan 1945) in Schleswig-Holstein. Its commander, *Vizeadmiral* Ernst Scheurien was k.i.a. on 8 Apr, succeeded by *Kapitän z S* Werner Hartmann and on 12 Apr by Army *Oberst* Graf Werner von Bassewitz-Levertzow. On 4 Apr it took up defensive positions on the Weser and Aller rivers north of Hanover, facing a major advance by British troops from VIII and XII Corps. It fought with unexpected ferocity at Rethem (11–12 Apr), Ostenholz and Winsen (13–14 Apr), and Groß Eilstorf and Kirchboitzen (14–15 Apr), delaying British advances and inflicting significant casualties. During 15–20 Apr it retreated into Bremen; from an initial strength of 12,372 men, only 1,815 then remained. By 23 Apr they had reached the North Sea coast at Cuxhaven, surrendering to British troops on 6 May 1945.

3rd Naval Infantry Division defended 'Fortress' Swinemünde (now Świnoujście, Poland) in the Sachsenhausen bridgehead from 1 Apr, before withdrawing to Lindow, north of Berlin, and surrendering to the Red Army near Kyritz on 8 May.

The **11th Naval Inf Div** was formed in the Netherlands (24 Mar 1945) from former depot bns, but disbanded on 8 May without seeing action. The same was true of **16th Naval Inf Div**, formed in March and disbanded on 12 April. **Naval Fortress Div Gotenhafen** was formed during Jan – Apr 1945 from ten Naval Rifle bns and four Naval AA bns, and saw action in the Gotenhafen–Danzig (now Gdynia–Gdańsk) Naval District. There were also two independent Naval Rifle Rgts (Copenhagen, Fünen) in Denmark; and nine Naval Rgts (Berger, Badermann, Gebauer, John, Zapp, Action Rgt 20, West 1–3) in France and Germany.

Naval depot units

In the *Reichsmarine,* recruits and replacements had carried out their basic training in Depot Bns (*Schiffsstammbataillone*) allocated to the North Sea or Baltic Sea Stations, grouped from 31 Mar 1935 in Depot Divisions (*Schiffsstammdivisionen*) commanded by the regional FOC's deputy (*2. Admiral*). A total of 31 depot bns would be formed, numbered 1.–28. & 30.–32., initially with even-numbered bns for the North Sea Station and odd-numbered for the Baltic Station. Most would be assembled into Depot Rgts (*Schiffsstammregimenter*). By Aug 1939, 14 Bns had been formed, numbered sequentially but grouped in 1st Depot Rgt (7., 9., 11. & 13. Bns) from Nov 1938; 2nd Rgt (8., 10., 1. & 14.) from 1 Oct 1937; plus 1.–6. independent battalions, which were subsequently posted as occupation troops to Denmark, Poland, Estonia, France, Belgium and the Netherlands.

More bns had been formed by 31 Dec 1943, allowing formation of 3rd Depot Rgt (7., 9., 11., 13., 15., 17. & 19. Bns) from Jan 1943; 4th Rgt (6., 10. & 24.) from Oct 1943; and 6th Rgt (8., 18. & 28. Bns) from December 1943. The 28. Bn was formed 15 Oct 1943 in Sennheim (now Cernay, Alsace) for European volunteers, and would disband in Wilhelmshaven in Oct 1944; 30. and 31. Bns, formed during July 1942, were reorganized as penal units (see below).

From 1 Jan 1944 the regiments were reorganized: 1st Rgt (1.–4. Bns); 2nd Rgt (14., 16., 20., 22. & 26.); 3rd Rgt (7., 9., 11., 13., 15., 17. & 19.); 4th Rgt (6., 10. & 24.); 5th Rgt (21., 23., 25. & 27.); and 6th Rgt (8., 18. & 28. Battalions). The 32. Bn was formed Oct 1944 from female naval volunteers. In all, seven depot bns (numbered 1., 6., 10., 14., 16., 20. & 27.) fought in the Naval Infantry Divs (see above) until May 1945, and eight (2.–4., 19., 21. & 22.–24.) as independent units.

Naval replacement units

Naval Replacement Bns (*Marine-Ersatz-Abteilungen* – MEAs) were formed, mainly on 1 Jan 1944, to replace Depot and other second-line battalions which had transferred to occupation duties abroad. A total of 36 MEAs were formed, mostly controlled by four Naval Replacement Regiments. The 1st Rgt (formed 1 Jan 1944) supervised 1., 3., 5., 7., 9., 11., 13., 15., 17., 19. & 21 Bns; 2nd Rgt (formed 1 Jan 1944), 2., 4., 6., 8., 10. & 12. Bns; 3rd Regt

Jan 1944: a Naval Artillery rating stands sentry in front of a gun position somewhere on the *Atlantikwall*. He wears the M1942 helmet and Navy field-grey uniform, the latter distinguished from the Army version by its pointed shoulder straps (for insignia, see commentaries to Plates G & H). His field-grey trousers are gathered by greenish-grey canvas webbing anklets. He carries the standard-issue *Karabiner 98k* bolt-action rifle, and wears black leather M1911 rifleman's belt equipment, apparently with an M1930 anti-gas sheet slung on his chest in its canvas pouch. (Bundesarchiv Bild 101II-299-1829-37, Frankreich, Atlantikwall, Posten vor Geschütz.jpg: Wikimedia Commons)

(Aug 1944), 31.–37. Bns; and 4th Rgt (Nov 1944), 6., 10., 12. & 22. Battalions. The 14., 16., 18., 22., 23., 25., 27., 28., 41.–43. & Athens Bns were independent units.

Naval NCO training units

In 1939 seamen were trained as NCOs in 1st–3rd Naval NCO Training Bns (*I–III Marine-Unteroffizier-Lehr-Abteilungen*), expanded on 1 Jan 1944 into 1st Naval Training Rgt (*1. Marine-Lehr-Regiment*) with four Naval Training Bns (*Marine-Lehr-Abteilungen*) numbered 1., 3., 5. & 7. This was disbanded in May 1945; 2nd Regt, with 3 bns (2., 4. & 6.), had already been disbanded in November 1944.

Naval penal units

On 25 May 1936 the Naval Special Battalion (*Marine-Sonderabteilung*) was formed as a penal unit to punish and rehabilitate personnel guilty of disciplinary offences. On 17 Oct 1939 the unit was reorganized as Wartime Special Bn East (*Kriegssonderabteilung Ost*) in Kiel, later on the Hela Peninsula in the Danzig Bight (now Gulf of Gdańsk, Poland). In July 1942 the bn was reformed as the Naval Field Special Company (*Marinefeldsonderkompanie* – MFSK), the 5th Coy of the Army's Field Special Bn on Hela. The rankers in this notorious company were brutally mistreated; in Feb 1943 it was transferred to MGK *Ost* as Naval Field Special Coy Hela Forest (*Wald-Hela*), and was disbanded on 3 Oct 1944.

In July 1942, 30. and 31. Depot Bns were formed in Wittmund, East Friesia, and Ventspils, Latvia, respectively, and immediately renamed Special Punishment Bns (*Sonder-Strafabteilungen*). Personnel who defied the disciplinary regime were transferred to the MFSK and joined Naval Action Command (MEA) North-West Russia (*Marine-Einsatz-Kommando Ostland*) fighting at Leningrad, but those who behaved well might be returned to service afloat. The unit disbanded on 22 Apr 1945.

Naval Anti-Aircraft Artillery machine-gunners practice firing their MG34 at aircraft from a dug-in position. Just visible on the gunner's M1940 field tunic is yellow braid collar edging, identifying his status as a junior NCO. His helmet still shows the eagle decal, officially discontinued on 28 Aug 1943. (Bundesarchiv, Bild 101II-M2KBK-196-35 / Wikimedia Commons)

NAVAL ARTILLERY

The Naval Artillery was the most important land branch of the Navy. During World War II its pillboxes, armoured or concrete turrets and bunkers would proliferate, defending ports and vulnerable stretches of coastline as Germany conquered increasing territory in Europe and North Africa (see Table 4, page 40).

From mobilization on 26 Aug 1939, the existing units were reorganized into about 107 *Marine-Artillerie-Abteiungen* (MAAs): 112., 114.–119., 132., 134., 141., 144. (not completed), 201.–205., Gascony (later 206., then 286.), 240., 242., 244., 260., 262., 264., 266., 280., Vendée (later 282.),

Gironde (later 284.), 301. (later Narvik, then 511.), 302. (later Trondheim, then 506.), 303. (later Bergen, then 504.), Zealand (later 308., then 508.), Jutland (later 309., then 509.), 500., Horten (later 501.), Kristiansand (later 502.), Stavanger (later 503.), Molde (later 505.), 507., 510.–514., 516.–518., 520.–525., 530.–537., 538. (not completed), 540. & 541., adding a 545. Bn in Mar 1945. Lighter MAAs were numbered 550., 601.–605., 607.–634., X (later 626.), 627., Y (later 628.), 629.–634. & 640. Eight such units (681.–688.) formed from Apr 1942 were deployed to the French Atlantic coast. At least one MAA was allocated to each Sea Defence Commander guarding the coasts of France, the Channel Islands, Belgium, the Netherlands, Germany, Denmark, Norway, Latvia, Estonia, Finland and Crimea.

Between Oct 1939 and Mar 1945, ten Naval Artillery Rgts (*Marine-Artillerie Regimenter* – MARs) were each formed from 2–3 existing MAAs, and numbered 1., 5., 10., 21., 22., 24., 30., 40., 41. & 50. These were deployed as independent units along the northern European coasts.

Naval anti-aircraft artillery

From 26 Aug 1939, 78 *Marine-Flakartillerie / Marine-Flak Abteilungen* (MFAs) were formed, numbered 200., 210.–217., 219., 221.–227., 229. (later 814.), 231.–236., 239., 241.–244., 246., 249., 251.–254., 256., 259., 261., 262., 264., 266., 271., 272., 274., 276., 281., 282., 284. (later 204.), 294., 704.–717., 720., 730., 801.– 813., & 815.–823.

5 May 1944: men of the Croatian Naval Legion parade on their return to Zagreb (compare with Plate F3). They wear standard German navy-blue uniforms, with the gold-lettered *'Kriegsmarine'* cap-tally. The right-hand rating shows the M1942 Crimea campaign shield above the two yellow chevrons of a *Matrosenobergefreiter,* but the Croatian checkered armshield and pinback Legion breast badge seem to have been removed, along with any branch and/ or trade badges. (Bundesarchiv Hrvatska pomorska legija.jpg)

OTHER LAND BRANCHES

Naval engineer units

From 26 Aug 1939 six Naval Construction Bns (*Marine-Bau-Bataillone*) numbered 311.–314., 316. and 323. were formed in Germany from the paramilitary National Labour Service (RAD). They were supplemented in 1942 by four bns numbered 321., 330., 340. and 360. for service on the Aegean and Black Sea coasts. In 1943–44 three Naval Construction Emergency Bns (*Marine-Bau-Bereitschaft-Abteilungen*), numbered 1.–3., were formed in Germany.

In December 1942 the ten construction bns were upgraded to Naval Fortress Engineer Bns (*Marine-Festungspionier-Bataillone*), stationed in occupied Europe. From 1942 eight Naval Fortress Engineer HQs – designated 1.–3., 6.–8., Adriatic, and Italy – were formed to supervise anti-invasion preparations in France, Italy and Germany. Additionally (as noted above), the 1st–3rd Naval Inf Divs each had a partly formed Engineer Bn (*Pionier-Bataillon*) carrying the divisional number.

Naval signals units

Between 1940 and 1944 four Naval Signals Bns (*Marine-Nachrichten-Abteilungen*) were formed, numbered 1.–3. (which would serve with 1st–3rd Naval Inf Divs) and 11. Three bns named *Nord*, *Oslo* and *West*, and 11 coys numbered 101.–106. and 121.–125., operated in Germany, France and Norway. Three Motorized Signal Bns numbered 1.–3. also operated on the Channel coast during 1941–44.

F

BLACK SEA & ENGLISH CHANNEL, 1942–43

(F1) *Oberfeldwebel*, **Sea Reconnaissance Group 125; Black Sea, autumn 1943**

This *Luftwaffe* senior NCO pilot in a *Seeaufklärungsgruppe* flies Arado Ar 196A-3 floatplanes. He wears the grey-blue Air Force officers' and senior NCOs' service dress tunic, with the 'universal' peaked field cap introduced on 11 June 1943. The normally open-collared tunic has its collar closed here for some semi-formal occasion, and he wears riding breeches and riding boots. The cap bears the silver *Luftwaffe* 'flying' version of the eagle-and-swastika *Hoheitsabzeichen*, above the cockade, both on a truncated triangular backing. The four-pocket tunic displays a larger silver breast eagle, and has silver-grey NCO edging-braid around the collar and shoulder straps. The collar patches, and the outer piping of the shoulder straps, are in the bright yellow of the flying branch. The patches bear this rank's four silver metal 'wings', and the straps its two silver 4-point stars. A holder of both classes of the Iron Cross, this airman displays the black and silver M1936 Pilots' Badge. His belt has a white-metal *Luftwaffe* eagle buckle-plate.

(F2) *Oberfähnrich*, **604th Naval Artillery Battalion; Guernsey, 1943**

In the peaceful occupied Channel Islands, this midshipman is on six months' probationary service before being commissioned as an officer. He wears an officers' peaked cap, field-grey service dress tunic, riding breeches and boots, but with a particular combination of insignia. The cap has a dark green band and piping, gold insignia, but silver chin cords. The tunic has a gold-wire breast eagle on dark green backing. Its collar patches show officers' silver-wire *Litzen* braids with yellow centre-stripes, separated by a white stripe; but the pointed field-grey shoulder straps have yellow NCO edge-braiding and bear two silver 4-point stars and the gold-metal winged flaming-shell-and-anchor branch badge. Both *Oberfähnrich* and *Fähnrich* Naval Artillery grades wore a yellow-thread winged shell on a dark green disc above both cuffs as a branch distinction.

(F3) *Kraftfahrhauptgefreiter*, **Croatian Naval Legion; Mariupol, Ukraine, August 1942**

This senior able seaman lorry-driver of the *Hrvatska Pomorska Legija* wears the German ratings' landing dress with the trousers rolled in the field. His grey-painted helmet still has the Navy's left-side decal. On his jumper is the German Navy's yellow breast eagle, and, high on the left breast, the Legion ratings' oval bronze badge of a chequered shield on a vertical anchor within a titled wreath; officers had a silver and white-enamel version. On his left upper sleeve is the red-and-white chequered national shield patch with the upper title 'HRVATSKA'; the latter might be omitted, while German cadre personnel displayed 'KROATIEN' instead. Below the patch this accomplished sailor wears the Automobile branch badge; three yellow cloth rank chevrons; and also a red ship-diver's trade badge. He has standard rifleman's belt equipment.

1

2

3

In 1939 the *Kriegsmarine* was prominent in the development of radar. Four Naval Radar Bns (*Marine-Funkmeß Abteilungen*) numbered 1.–4. were formed Nov 1941–Sept 1944, followed by 13 independent Radar Coys numbered 41., 42., 51., 61.–64., 81., 82., 91., 101., 102. & 110., dispersed over occupied territory.

Naval air warning service

Nine Naval Air-Raid Warning Bns (*Marine-Flugmelde-Abteilungen*) – designated 1.–3., 5., 7., North Friesia, West Baltic, Pillau and Pomeranian Coast – maintained surveillance over the Channel and Baltic coasts. They were supplemented by volunteers in two Naval Signal Female Auxiliary Bns (*Marine-Nachrichtenhelferinnen-Abteilungen* 1. & 2.).

Naval motor transport units

Between Feb 1941 and June 1944, 21 Naval Motor Transport Bns (*Marine-*

TABLE 4: Selective battle order of Navy Land Forces, 1 Sept 1939–8 May 1945

NAVAL INFANTRY

Naval Brigade Weber (Bordeaux, France, Aug–Sept 1944): Nav Rgts von Pflugk-Harttung, Badermann, Kühnemann.
Naval Rifle Bde Nord (Husum, Germany, Nov 1944): Nav Rifle Rgts 1–4, Nav Rifle Bns 301–316; **became 1. Naval Inf Div.**

1. Naval Inf Div (Stettin, 31 Jan–4 May 1945): Nav Rifle Rgts 1–4, each two bns (24 Feb 1945); Nav Fusilier Bn 1 (24 Feb–Mar 1945); Nav Arty Rgt 1 (1 bn); Nav AT Bn 1 (Army); Nav Eng Bn 1 (22 Feb 1945); Nav Sigs Bn 1 (15 Apr 1945); Nav Field Replacement Bn 1 (Mar 1945); Nav Med Coy 1 (Feb 1945).
2. Naval Inf Div (Schleswig-Holstein, 31 Jan–8 May 1945): Nav Gren Rgts 5–7 (each two bns); Nav Fusilier Bn 2; Nav Arty Rgt 2; Nav AT Bn 2; Nav Eng Bn 2; Nav Sigs Bn 2; Nav Field Replacement Bn 2; Nav Supply Rgt 200.
3. Naval Inf Div (Pomerania, 1 Apr–8 May 1945): Nav Gren Rgts 8–10; Nav Fusilier Bn 3 (21 Apr 1945); Nav Rifles Bns 126 & 128; Nav Arty Rgt 3; div support units.
11. Naval Inf Div (Netherlands, 24 Mar–8 May 1945): Nav Rifle Rgts 111–113.
16. Naval Inf Div (Netherlands, Mar 1945): Nav Rifle Rgts 161–163.

Naval Rifle Rgts: Copenhagen (Denmark, 1945); Fünen (Denmark, Apr 1945).
Naval Rgts: Berger (Narvik, Norway, Apr–July 1940); Badermann (Bordeaux, Aug–Sept 1944); Gebauer (Dax, France, Aug–Sept 1944); John (La Rochelle, France, Aug 1944); Zapp (La Rochelle, Sept 1944); Nav Action Rgt 20 (Wilhelmshafen, Mar 1945); West 1–3 (Emden, Apr 1945).

NAVAL ARTILLERY RGTS

1. Rgt (Belle Île, Brittany, Apr 1942); 5. Rgt (Baltiysk, E. Prussia, Oct 1939–Jan 1940); 10. Rgt (Liepāja, Latvia, Nov 1944); 21. Rgt (The Hague, Netherlands, May–June 1940); 22. Rgt (Le Coq de Haen, Netherlands, May–June 1940); 24. Rgt (Calais, France, May–July 1940); 26. Rgt (Brest, France, July 1940); 30. Rgt (Harstadt, Norway, Jan 1945); 40. Rgt (Frederikshavn, Denmark, Nov 1944); 41. Rgt (Copenhagen, Nov 1944); 50. Rgt (Świnoujście, Poland, Mar 1945).

NAVAL ANTI-AIRCRAFT ARTILLERY RGTS

1. Rgt (Jan 1940), **became I Naval AA Bde** (Baltic, May 1942–Nov 1944); **2. Rgt** (Jan 1940), **became II Naval AA Bde** (May 1942–Nov 1944); **24. Rgt** (Brest), **became III Naval AA Bde** (Brest, Apr 1943); **20. Rgt** (Brittany), **became IV Naval AA Bde** (Brest, Apr 1943); **22. Rgt, became V Naval AA Bde** (St Nazaire, France, Apr 1943); **Naval Shipborne AA Bde North** (Mar 1942–Jan.1945).

3. Rgt (Świnoujście, Mar 1945); 6. Rgt (Emden, Mar 1942–Nov 1944); 8. Rgt (Brunsbüttel, Mar 1940), became 14. Regt; 8. Rgt (Feb 1941–Apr 1943); 9. Rgt (Gotenhafen/ Gdynia, Poland, Sept–Dec 1942–Dec 1944); 14. Rgt (Westerland, Mar 1940–Nov 1944); 20. Rgt (Lorient, France, Aug 1941–Apr 1944). 22. Rgt (St Nazaire, Nov 1941–Apr 1943); 24. Rgt (Brest, Dec 1941–Apr 1943); 30. Rgt (Narvik, May 1942–Apr 1944); 31. Rgt (Bergen, Norway, June–Nov 1940–Apr 1944); 32. Rgt (Trondheim, Norway, Oct 1944).

DEPOT UNITS

Ship Depot Rgts (Baltic Sea): 1. Rgt (Stralsund, Nov 1938–Jan 1944); **3. Rgt** (Epinal, France, Jan 1943–Oct 1944); **5. Rgt** (Pillau/ Baltiysk, Russia, Jan 1944–Feb 1945).
Ship Depot Rgts (North Sea): 2. Rgt (Beverloo, Belgium, Oct 1943–Jan 1944); **4. Rgt** (Groningen, Netherlands, Oct 1943–Mar 1945); **6. Rgt** (Belfort, France, Dec 1943–Sept 1944).

Ship Depot Battalions (Baltic Sea): 2. Bn (Wilhelmshaven, June 1937–Jan 1944); **4. Bn** (Stralsund, May 1938–May 1945); **6. Bn** (Steenwijk, Netherlands, Apr 1941–Mar 1945); **8. Bn** (Besançon, France, Jan–Nov 1944); **10. Bn** (Assens, Netherlands, Jan 1944–Mar 1945); **12. Bn** (Brake, Belgium, Jan 1941–Feb 1942); **14. Bn** (Breda, Netherlands, Sept 1940–Mar 1945); **16. Bn** (Gotenhafen, June 1940–Mar 1945); **18. Bn** (Belfort, France, Oct 1940–Feb 1945); **20. Bn** (Ede, Netherlands, June 1941–Mar 1945); **22. Bn** (Beverloo, July 1943–Mar 1945); **24. Bn** (Groningen, Netherlands, Jan 1944–Mar 1945); **26. Bn** (Wezep, Netherlands, Aug 1943–Sept 1944); **28. Bn** (Sennheim, Alsace, Oct 1943–Oct 1944); **30. Bn** (Wittmund, July 1942–Apr 1945); **32. Bn** (Wyk am Föhr, Oct 1943–Dec 1944).

Ship Depot Bns (North Sea): 1. Bn (Kiel, Oct 1938); **3. Bn** (Eckernförde, Apr 1938–Mar 1945); **5. Bn** (Epinal, France, Apr 1943–Jan 1944); **7. Bn** (Stralsund, Apr 1938); **9. Bn** (St Die, France, Jan–Oct 1944); **11. Bn** (Bruyères, France , Jan–Oct. 1944); **13. Bn** (Gerardmer, France, Nov 1943–Oct 1944); **15. Bn** (Epinal, Apr 1941–Oct. 1944); **17. Bn** (Metz, France, Aug 1941–Nov 1944); **19. Bn** (Hanstedt, Denmark, July 1942– 1944); **21. Bn** (Memel/ Klaipeda, Lithuania, Jan–Oct 1944); **23. Bn** (Deutsch Krone, Jan 1944–Mar 1945); **25. Bn** (Pillau, Jan 1944–Mar 1945); **27. Bn** (Otterup, Denmark, Jan 1944–Apr 1945); **31. Bn** (Narva, Estonia, July 1942–Apr 1945).

Kraftfahr-Abteilungen) were formed in Germany and occupied Europe, numbered 1., 3.–6., 8.–10., 12., 14., 16.–20., 22., 24., 26., 28., 32. & 34. These were supplemented in 1942 by 1st–4th Naval Lorry Operational Bns (*1.–4. Marine-Kraftwagen-Einsatz-Abteilungen*) for transporting ammunition and other heavy loads, plus a 5th Bn in 1944. In Oct 1944 3rd and 5th Bns were re-formed as the 4-bn Naval Motorized K-Regt 1 (*Marine-K.-Regiment (motoriziert) 1*), to support the naval special forces (see page 31).

Naval guard units

To guard vulnerable localities, during 1939–45 at least 13 battalions were formed in Germany. These included a Naval Territorial Bn (*Marine-Landeschützen-Abteilung*), 1939; 1.–3. Channel Guard Bns (*Kanal-Wach-Abteilungen*), Mar 1940; Coastal Monitoring Bn (*Küstenüberwachungs-Abteilung*), 1942–Mar 1944; and 1. & 2. Transport Escort Bns (*Transport-Begleit-Bataillone*), Sept–Nov 1944. At least 3,800 personnel of 604., 605., 608. & 610. Naval Security Bns (*Marine-Sicherungs-Bataillone*) were posted in Oct 1944 from the Aegean to Kosovo to replace deserters from the Albanian *21. Waffen-Gebirgs Div der SS 'Skanderbeg'*. Two units raised in 1945 were the Dönitz Guard Bn (*Wach-Bataillon Dönitz*) in Feb, and 165. Naval Guard Battalion.

FOREIGN VOLUNTEERS

German recruitment of foreign volunteers into the Navy was unsystematic, and only about 10,000 men actually joined. From 2 July 1941 the OKW allowed Dutch and Swedish volunteers to enlist, but no further details are available. In 1944 German Army-style national armshield patches were prescribed for the Navy, but there is no evidence that they were ever issued, in spite of the existence of a poster publicizing Dutch volunteers.

Croatia

The Croatian Naval Legion (*Hrvatska Pomorska Legija*), officially the Croatian Naval Battalion – Black Sea (*Hrvatski Pomorski Sklop – Crno More*), was formed in July 1941 with 343 men (23 officers, 220 NCOs and 100 ratings), and assigned to the German Navy. After training in Varna, Bulgaria, the Legion carried out duties on Ukraine's Black Sea coast as 23rd Minesweeper Flotilla, defending Heniscek, Ukraine, from Sept 1941. In May 1942 the flotilla, now including some German and Ukrainian sailors, transferred to Mariupol. In Mar 1943 two Croatian Naval Artillery batteries joined the Legion, bringing strength up to more than 1,000 men. In Oct 1943 the Legion began its return to Croatia, completed on 21 May 1944. Most personnel then joined the Croatian Navy, but the Naval Arty deployed to Split in Feb 1944 under German command.

Spain

A group of Spanish Navy volunteers accompanied the Army 'Blue Division' to Russia during 1942–43, forming three task forces (*Comisiónes*). Of these, the *1a 'Fernandez Martin'* patrolled the Baltic around Kotka, Finland, 13 Feb 1942–7 Mar 1943 with four flotillas: 1st Mine Clearance, 3rd Minesweeper, 3rd Patrol Boat, and 12th Submarine-Hunter. The *2a 'Fernandez de la Puente'* served with the Eastern Minesweeper Flotilla, and *3a 'Urzaiz'* with 9th Speed Boat Flotilla, until July 1943.

Vizeadmiral Günther Lütjens wearing navy-blue service dress; note the broad 'notched' open collar, the placing of the top pair of gold buttons, and the deep rectangular hip-pocket flaps. Promoted *Admiral* on 1 Sept 1939, Lütjens was given command of the battleship *Bismarck*; he went down with his ship on 27 May 1941. (Bundesarchiv Bild 101II-MW-0434-05A)

Foreign guard units

Three volunteer guard units were formed, all wearing navy-blue German uniforms. In early 1941 a Danish Civil Guard (*Zivilvægtere*) was formed, and later the 1,500-strong Naval Guard (*Marinevægtere*). From early 1943, 250–300 French volunteers guarded submarines in La Pallice near La Rochelle, wearing a French tricolour shield on the right upper sleeve. A unit of French Naval Guardsmen (*Kriegsmarine-Wehrmänner*) served in other German bases on the French coast.

UNIFORMS

NAVY-BLUE UNIFORMS

The uniforms worn depended on the order of dress; the rank-classes – of officers, senior NCOs, junior NCOs and ratings; and the branch to which the man belonged.[4]

Full Dress (*Große Uniform*). A 19th-century officers' uniform sometimes still worn on ceremonial occasions, particularly abroad, but seldom after the outbreak of war. It comprised a black cocked hat; white shirt with stiff upright collar and black bow-tie; knee-length navy-blue frock coat, with rank both on epaulettes or shoulder straps and cuffs; medals; trousers with gold braid stripes; silver braid belt and sword-knot; sword; white gloves.

Parade Dress (*Paradeanzug*). Introduced 1939 for parades in presence of senior officers or political leaders, for funerals and for guards of honour. *Officers and senior NCOs*: Navy-blue peaked cap; white shirt, black tie; service tunic with cuff rank insignia; medals; breeches; black leather riding boots and sword-knot; silver brocade belt; sword; grey leather gloves. *Junior NCOs and ratings*: Sailors' navy-blue peakless cap; blue or white jumper with sailors' light blue wide collar, black silk scarf; short, open parade jacket with sleeve rank insignia, medals; blue or white trousers (sometimes contrasting with the jumper) over black leather marching

---

4 See further details throughout Plate commentaries. Since mess-dress order is not illustrated in this book, it is omitted from the text below.

'Navy-blue' indicates an almost black shade. In this text 'gold', 'silver' and 'bronze' refer simply to the colours of metals and metallic-wire thread used for insignia. 'Yellow' in Navy insignia was a strong *goldgelb*, like the Army's *Waffenfarbe* for cavalry. 'Eagle' cap and right-breast insignia refers to the Nazi national *Hoheitsabzeichen* of a spread-winged eagle with a wreathed swastika in its talons. The eagle depicted in many other Army and Navy insignia had down-folded wings, giving a 'hunched' effect. Circular tricolour *Reich* cap cockades were black/ white/ red centre; they were three-dimensional in the wreathed presentation on officers' and senior NCOs' peaked service caps and on officers' on-board caps, and flat machine-woven on junior ranks' caps.

The pullover upper garment of the ratings' basic blue and white uniforms is referred to as a 'jumper', following the British and American term. Navy-blue 'service tunics' were double-breasted jackets with open lapels, two rows of five gold front buttons, an open-top internal left breast pocket, and rectangular external flaps for internal hip pockets. Field-grey tunics were of Army pattern, single-breasted with five or six front buttons, stand-and-fall collars usually worn closed, and four external patch pockets.

boots; a black belt with yellow-metal buckle-plate, black ammunition pouches and bayonet frog, and rifle.

Formal Ceremonial Dress (*Großer Gesellschaftsanzug*). Worn by officers on special festive occasions, including e.g. weddings. Navy-blue peaked cap; white shirt with stiff standing collar, black bow-tie; frock coat with shoulder-strap and cuff rank insignia; medals; trousers (sometimes with gold braid stripes), black leather shoes, ceremonial belt; gold aiguillettes and sword-knot; white gloves.

Informal Ceremonial Dress (*Kleiner Gesellschaftsanzug*). As formal ceremonial dress but with medal ribbons only.

Service Dress (*Dienstanzug*). Worn for public occasions not requiring parade dress. *Officers*: Navy-blue peaked cap; frock coat (later service tunic); medals or miniature medals; trousers; sword or dagger; silver brocade belt, sword-knot or dagger-knot; grey leather gloves. *Senior NCOs*: Navy-blue peaked cap; service tunic; dagger and knot; grey leather gloves. *Junior NCOs and ratings*: Peakless sailors' cap; short parade jacket; navy-blue jumper, light blue sailors' wide collar, black silk scarf; navy-blue trousers.

Undress Uniform (*Kleiner Dienstanzug*). Worn for daily duties on board ship, off duty, and for infantry or landing training. *Officers and senior NCOs*: Navy-blue peaked-cap, tunic and trousers, white shirt, black tie; grey leather gloves. *Junior NCOs*: Navy-blue peakless sailor's cap; navy-blue jumper, sailor's light blue wide collar with black silk scarf; navy-blue trousers; black leather marching boots. *Ratings*: The same, with black leather belt and rifle equipment when appropriate.

Walking-Out Dress (*Ausgehanzug*). *Officers*: Navy-blue peaked-cap, initially frock coat and shirt with stiff standing collar; in wartime, service tunic, white shirt and black tie, navy-blue trousers; black shoes; sometimes dagger and knot (from 1940); grey leather gloves. *Senior NCOs*: Navy-

Kommodore Friedrich-Oskar Ruge inspects sailors of a minesweeper flotilla, 1941; note the single broad cuff-ring of this rank, adopted on 3 Mar 1939. The three ratings (right) in walking-out dress wear the *Überzieher* pea-jacket with plain cornflower-blue collar patches. The details of the peakless sailors' cap might vary; note here the differing crown sizes, and the very long black silk tally-ribbons. Only one of these men wears the 31 Aug 1940 Minesweeper War Badge, normally awarded after three operational sorties; crews of submarine-chasers and escort vessels were also eligible for this badge. (Bundesarchiv Bild 10II-MW-2064-15A, Friedrich Oskar Ruge bei MS-Flottille.jpg / Wikimedia Commons)

Detail from photo of sailors being inspected on the Channel coast in Sept 1941. Note the large customized cap crown, the light blue sailors' collar with three white edging-stripes, and the Narvik campaign shield. Below this is the gold NCOs' anchor, here with an unidentified branch badge superimposed. (Bundesarchiv Bild 10II-MW-2789-10, Kanalküste, Inspektion Hermann v.Fischel.jpg)

blue peaked cap, tunic and trousers; white shirt, black tie; dagger and knot; grey leather gloves. *Junior NCOs and ratings*: Navy-blue peakless sailors' cap, jumper and trousers; light blue sailor's wide collar, black silk scarf; navy-blue short parade jacket or pea-jacket; grey leather gloves.

Blue Landing Dress (*Blauer Landungsanzug*). Worn for exercises on land and infantry manoeuvres in winter (1 Oct–19 Apr). *Officers and senior NCOs*; Steel helmet, or on-board cap (*Bordmütze*, nicknamed *Schiffchen*, 'little ship', and similar pattern to the *Luftwaffe Fliegermütze*); navy-blue tunic with cuff rank insignia; white shirt and black tie; navy-blue breeches and black riding boots (NCOs, trousers and leggings); brown leather service belt with crossbrace (abolished 1940), pistol. *Junior NCOs and ratings*: Steel helmet, navy-blue jumper, sailors' light-blue wide collar and black silk scarf; navy-blue trousers with black leather marching boots or leggings; black leather belt, Y-straps and rifle equipment; rifle.

WHITE UNIFORMS

White Tropical Service Dress (*Weißer Tropenanzug*). Worn abroad as Service and Undress Uniform on board ship, and sometimes in Germany as summer day uniform. *Officers and senior NCOs*: White peaked or on-board cap or tropical helmet; white M1937 single-breasted, open-collar, four-pocket tunic; white shirt and black tie; gold metal pinback breast eagle (sometimes also worn on brown tropical dress); shoulder-strap rank insignia; white trousers, shoes and gloves; sword or dagger with knot, sometimes ceremonial belt. *Junior NCOs and ratings*: White sailors' peakless or on-board cap or tropical helmet; white jumper, with white-striped light blue cuffs and wide sailors' collar, black silk scarf; white trousers and black boots.

White Landing Dress (*Weißer Landungsanzug*). Worn for exercises on land and infantry manoeuvres in summer (20 Apr–30 Sept). *Officers and senior NCOs*: Steel helmet; white tunic with shoulder-strap rank insignia; white or navy-blue shirt, black tie; white breeches and black riding boots (NCOs, white trousers and leggings); brown leather service belt with pistol. *Junior NCOs and ratings*: Steel helmet, white fatigue jumper, sailors' light blue wide collar and black silk scarf; white fatigue trousers with black leather marching boots or leggings and ankle boots; belt and rifle equipment; rifle.

BROWN UNIFORMS

Barracks Service Dress (*Innendienstanzug*) *for officers and senior NCOs.* Light brown (or navy-blue) peaked cap; an open-collared four-pocket light brown service tunic with shoulder-strap rank insignia; white shirt and black tie; light brown trousers over black shoes. *(continued on page 46)*

(continued on page 46)

TABLE 5: Line rank insignia, 17 Oct 1936–8 May 1945

Admirale (*Flag officers*):

Rank *Royal Navy equivalent*	Gold braid cuff insignia, below 5-point gold star Line branch badge	Shoulder strap rank insignia; navy-blue underlay for all ranks
Großadmiral (1) *Admiral of the Fleet*	4 medium rings, above 1 thick ring	Crossed silver batons on gold/ silver/ gold interwoven-cord straps
Generaladmiral als Oberbefehlshaber der Kriegsmarine (2) *(Senior) Admiral as C-in-C Navy*	4 medium rings, above 1 thick ring	3 silver 4-point stars on gold/ silver/ gold interwoven-cord straps
Generaladmiral *(Senior) Admiral*	3 medium rings, above 1 thick ring	3 silver 4-point stars on gold/ silver/ gold interwoven-cord straps
Admiral *Admiral*	3 medium rings, above 1 thick ring	2 silver 4-point stars on gold/ silver/ gold interwoven-cord straps
Vizeadmiral *Vice Admiral*	2 medium rings, above 1 thick ring	1 silver 4-point star on gold/ silver/ gold interwoven-cord straps.
Konteradmiral *Rear Admiral*	1 medium ring, above 1 thick ring	Gold/ silver/ gold interwoven-cord straps

Stabsoffiziere (*Senior Line officers*):

Kapitän zur See und Kommodore (3) *Commodore*	4 medium rings	2 gold 4-point stars on silver plaited- cord straps
Kapitän zur See *Captain*	4 medium rings	2 gold 4-point stars on silver plaited- cord straps
Fregattenkapitän *(Senior) Commander*	4 medium rings **(4)**	1 gold 4-point star on silver plaited- cord straps
Korvettenkapitän *Commander*	3 medium rings	Silver plaited-cord straps

Kapitänleutnante & Leutnante (*Junior Line officers*):

Kapitänleutnant *Lieutenant-Commander*	1 medium, above 1 thin, above 1 medium rings	2 gold 4-point stars on flat silver-cord straps
Oberleutnant zur See *Lieutenant*	2 medium rings	1 gold 4-point star on flat silver-cord straps
Leutnant zur See *Sub-Lieutenant*	1 medium ring	Flat silver-cord straps

Unteroffiziere mit Portepee (*Senior Line non-commissioned officers*):

Rank *Royal Navy equivalent*	–	Shoulder-strap rank insignia
Oberwaffenwart (5) *(Senior) Warrant Officer*	–	3 silver 4-point stars, gold crossed anchor & cannon, and chevron, on navy-blue straps with gold braid edging
Waffenwart (6) *Warrant Officer*	–	2 silver 4-point stars; gold crossed anchor & cannon, on navy-blue straps with gold braid edging
Stabsoberbootsmann (7) *(Senior) Chief Petty Officer*	–	3 silver 4-point stars on navy-blue straps with gold braid edging
Hauptfeldwebel (8) *Company Sergeant Major*	Doubled gold braid cuff rings	2 gold 4-point stars on narrow, flat silver-cord straps
Oberfähnrich zur See (9) *Midshipman*	5-point gold star Line branch badge	2 gold 4-point stars on narrow, flat silver-cord straps
Oberbootsmann *Chief Petty Officer*	–	2 silver 4-point stars on navy-blue straps with gold braid edging
Bootsmann *Petty Officer*	–	1 silver 4-point star on navy-blue straps with gold braid edging

Unteroffiziere ohne Portepee (*Junior Line non-commissioned officers*):

Rank *Royal Navy equivalent*	Insignia on left upper sleeve	Braid bars on blue collar patches; Fähnrich's shoulder straps
Oberbootsmannsmaat *(Senior) Leading Seaman*	Gold fouled anchor above gold chevron	2 gold bars on collar patches
Fähnrich zur See (11) *Sea Cadet*	5-point star branch badge	Narrow, flat silver-cord straps
Bootsmannsmaat *Leading Seaman*	Gold fouled anchor	1 gold bar on collar patches

(continued overleaf)

Mannschaften (*Ratings*):

Rank *Royal Navy equivalent*	5-point gold star Line branch badge and chevron/s on left upper sleeve	–
Matrosenstabsgefreiter (12) *Able Seaman (8 years' service)*	5-point star above gold 4-point star and 2 gold plaited chevrons	–
Matrosenobergefreiter (13) *Able Seaman (6 years' service)*	5-point star branch badge above gold 4-point star and 1 gold plaited chevron	–
Oberstabsmatrose (14) *Able Seaman (4.5 years' service)*	5-point star above 3 gold chevrons	–
Stabsmatrose (15) *Able Seaman (2 years' service)*	5-point star above 2 gold chevrons	–
Obermatrose (16) *Able Seaman*	5-point star above 1 gold chevron	–
Matrose (17) *Ordinary Seaman*	5-point star	–

Notes numbered above:
(1) Rank held only by Raeder (from 1 Apr 1939) & Dönitz (from 30 Jan 1943).
(2) Appointment held only by Raeder (20 Apr 1936–1 Apr 1939).
(3) 'K z S als Kommodore' was 1933 appointment held by officer commanding his own and several other ships; flag officers' cap peak braid. (13 Mar 1939) became 'Kommodore'; substituted single thick cuff ring, added flag officers' greatcoat lapel-facings.
(4) (1 Aug 1940), substituted 3 medium cuff rings; (25 Feb 1944) substituted 1 medium above 1 thin above 2 medium rings.
(5) Rank introduced (1 Oct 1938) for Waffenwart with 6 years' service.
(6) Technical-branch rank introduced (25 June 1934) for Obermechaniker with 3 years' service. (1 Oct 1938) classed as equivalent to Stabsmechaniker; after 3 years, promotable to Oberwaffenwart.
(7) In technical branches (16 Feb 1939), Stabsmechaniker re-titled Stabsobermechaniker.
(8) (5 Nov 1938) re-titling of the senior NCO in a Land Forces company, from previous Kompaniefeldwebel.
(9) Senior cadet qualified as officer but serving 6 months' practical training aboard ship.
(10) Grades of Stabsbootsmann & Stabsbootsmann (F) instituted (1 Oct 1938), the latter for men who had signed on for 12 years' service.
(11) Officer cadet with 1 year's service.
(12) Former Imperial Navy rating with 8 years' service, unpromotable to junior NCO rank (17 Oct 1936). Retitled Matrosenstabsgefreiter alter Art (31 Jan 1938), and Matrosenoberstabsgefreiter (23 July 1940).
(13) Rating with 6 years' service, unpromotable to junior NCO rank (17 Oct 1936). Retitled Matrosenobergefreiter alter Art (31 Jan 1938), and Matrosenstabsgefreiter neuer Art (23 July 1940).
(14) Rating with 4½ years' service, possibly promotable to junior NCO rank (17 Oct 1936). Retitled Matrosenhauptgefreiter (31 Jan 1938).
(15) Rating with 2 years' service, possibly promotable to junior NCO rank (17 Oct 1936). Retitled Matrosenobergefreiter (31 Jan 1938).
(16) Possibly promotable to junior NCO rank (17 Oct 1936). Retitled Matrosengefreiter (31 Jan 1938).
(17) Recruit, possibly promotable to junior NCO rank (17 Oct 1936).

Brown Tropical Dress (*Brauner Tropenuniform*). This uniform in light brown cloth or cord was introduced in Dec 1941 for service in the Mediterranean, North Africa, southern Europe and the tropics. *Officers:* Light brown (or white-covered) peaked cap; light brown single-breasted four-pocket tunic with open collar; shoulder-strap rank insignia; light brown shirt, black tie; light brown riding breeches and black leather riding boots; brown leather service

NAVAL LAND FORCES, 1942–44
(G1) *Flugmeldeobergefreiter*, **5th Air Warning Battalion; Pillau, 1944**
This senior able seaman in Germany wears the field-grey M1942 field uniform with the M1943 *Einheitsfeldmütze* and an M1942 greatcoat. The cap has a yellow thread eagle above the cockade on a single backing, and two grey-painted pebbled buttons on the turn-down flap; the greatcoat also has painted pebbled buttons. Field-grey pointed shoulder straps bear the Air Warning Service branch badge of winged lightning flashes above crossed anchors, and yellow NCO braid rank chevrons are worn on field-grey backing on the left sleeve.

(G2) *Oberstleutnant*, **360th' Construction Battalion; Brittany, 1942**
Although under Navy command, this lieutenant-colonel battalion commander wears Army field-grey field uniform with black Engineer branch distinctions. His cap has silver-wire insignia and chin cords, and black piping. His tunic has the M1935 dark green collar, the patches bearing silver *Litzen*

with black centre-stripes. His breast eagle is of silver wire on dark green backing. The shoulder straps of plaited light grey cord have black underlay, and a single gold 4-point rank star, but no Navy branch badge.

(G3) *Marinefestungspionierstabsoberfeldwebel*, **3rd Naval Fortress Engineer HQ; Aurich, October 1944**
This tongue-twisting multi-syllabic compound service/ branch/ rank/ title identifies a senior chief petty officer Fortress Engineer. Based in Germany, he wears field-grey M1935 field uniform with an M1942 field cap. The cap has separate yellow eagle and tricolour cockade insignia. The service tunic has M1943 standard collar insignia, comprising two matt grey bars with light grey (rather than branch-colour) centre-stripes. The only noticeable Navy features are five (later sometimes six) gold 'anchor' front buttons; the Navy belt buckle; the yellow breast eagle; and yellow NCO braid around the collar edges and inside the Army's black Engineer piping around the shoulder straps, which bear three 4-point rank stars arranged in a triangle. A dark green oval patch on his left forearm shows the yellow-thread 'Fp' of the *Festungspioniere*.

belt (omitted for Walking Out Dress), and holstered pistol reversed on left hip. *NCOs and ratings:* Light brown peaked tropical field cap, on-board cap or tropical helmet; light brown field tunic (*senior NCOs*, shoulder straps with rank insignia and blue edging; *junior NCOs*, blue chevrons on left upper sleeve); light brown shirt and black tie; light brown trousers, black leather ankle boots; brown webbing tropical belt. Alternatively, all ranks might wear a light brown open-neck shirt, shorts and knee-socks, or the Army-style field-grey greatcoat.

FATIGUE UNIFORMS

Grey Fatigue Dress (*Grauer Arbeitsanzug*). *Officers and senior NCOs* wore a navy-blue on-board cap, light grey open-collar service tunic with shoulder-strap rank insignia, white shirt and black tie, light grey trousers and black leather shoes.

White Fatigue Dress (*Weißer Arbeitsanzug*). *Junior NCOs* wore a navy-blue on-board cap, white open-collar fatigue tunic with left upper sleeve rank insignia, white trousers and black leather ankle boots. *Ratings* wore a white on-board cap and fatigue jumper, sailors' light blue wide collar and black silk scarf; white trousers and black leather ankle boots.

Submarine Fatigue Dress (*U-Boot Päckchen*). *Officers and senior NCOs* wore a navy-blue peaked cap; light greenish-grey open-collared waist-length blouse (or, often, captured British Army brown 'denim battledress'), sometimes with shoulder-strap rank insignia, and matching trousers. *Junior NCOs and ratings* wore a navy-blue on-board cap, and the same fatigues, sometimes with white-metal 'chevrons' on the collar points in imitation of braid. Footwear was black leather ankle or seaboots, or light canvas-topped shoes. At sea, garments from different clothing issues were often worn mixed. (For U-boat protective clothing, see under Plate D3.)

Summer 1939: personnel in white summer service uniforms. The officer (left) wears an M1939 white-covered cork tropical helmet with a small gold-metal one-piece eagle, swastika and cockade badge. His six-button M1933 closed-collar tunic has a gold-metal pinback breast eagle, and shoulder straps of rank, and his trousers hang straight over white shoes. The other officer (third left) wears the M1937 five-button open-collar tunic, with a white shirt and black tie. The ratings wear white-covered peakless caps; white service-dress jumpers with pointed light blue cuffs trimmed at the top with two white stripes, and at the bottom with a single edge-stripe; the wide light blue sailors' collar with black silk scarf; white trousers, and black boots. An alternative order of dress was white jumpers with navy-blue trousers. (Courtesy Jean-Yves Goffi Collection)

FIELD-GREY UNIFORMS

Flag officers initially wore a peaked cap with a field-grey crown, dark green band and plain black leather peak; a gold-wire eagle above a gold-wreathed cockade; gold chin cords, and gold piping to the crown seam and band edges (the piping changing to dark green from 26 May 1943). The M1935 Naval field-grey (*feldgrau*) field tunic replaced the Army-pattern tunic from 31 Oct 1935. For flag officers its dark-green closed collar bore gold-wire *Larisch* embroidery on cornflower-blue patches; they wore shoulder straps of rank, and a gold-wire breast eagle. Grey (from 1940, field-grey) riding breeches had cornflower-blue seam-piping flanked by two matching stripes (*Lampassen*), worn with black leather riding boots. The service belt and holster were brown leather. The field-grey greatcoat had a dark-green collar, and lapels opening to show cornflower-blue internal facing.

Other officers' dark-green tunic collars bore double silver 'Guards braid' *Litzen* with yellow centre-stripes, separated by a white stripe; they wore shoulder straps of their rank, grey-painted buttons embossed with an anchor, and plain breeches. NCOs wore field-grey uniform initially with a dark-green collar and pointed shoulder straps; from 1940 both became field-grey, and later in the war the shoulder straps became rounded. Their collar patches bore narrow light grey *Litzen*; senior NCOs had yellow braid edging to the collar itself and to their shoulder straps of rank. Junior NCOs and ratings lacked this edging, and wore left-sleeve rank insignia. Trousers were initially grey, but field-grey from 1940, and worn with short-shaft black marching boots. Headgear was the M1935, M1938 or M1942 Army-pattern peakless

ABOVE LEFT
Detail from photo of the funeral of German sailors killed at the Battle of the River Plate, Dec 1939. These ratings from the crew of *Admiral Graf Spee* are wearing the combination of white service-dress jumpers with navy-blue trousers. (Hans Langsdoff / Wikimedia Commons)

ABOVE RIGHT
Summer 1939: ratings wearing M1911 rifleman's black leather belt equipment presenting arms on board ship. Their peakless caps have white summer covers; they wear plain white fatigue jumpers with wide light blue sailors' collars, and white trousers. (Courtesy Christopher Harrod Collection)

North Africa, 1942: two officers (at right, a *Kapitänleutnant*) consulting ship's charts. They are wearing brown shirts and black ties under the four-pocket brown tropical service tunic, with shoulder straps of rank, woven or embroidered gold breast eagles, and decorations. The pinback metal breast eagle from white tropical dress was sometimes substituted. (Bundesarchiv Bild 101II-MS-0986-10, Nordafrika, Offiziere beim K / Wikimedia Commons)

field cap or later the M1943 peaked field cap. The black leather belt had a yellow-metal buckle-plate.

Naval Engineer Construction Bns and Fortress Engineers wore the field-grey Army Engineer uniform with the M1935 NCO peaked cap or field caps; silver braid NCOs' collar and shoulder-strap edging, and silver breast eagles.

RANKS & RANK INSIGNIA

(See also Table 5, pages 45–46)

Below the officers' three rank classes, the Navy's rank titles were greatly complicated by the elision of ranks as such, with words identifying branches, qualification grades/ seniority-in-service within particular branches – and by 1939, given the character of its Land Forces, also by some convergence with German Army ranks. Given the German practice of coining multi-syllabic compound words, this produced some titles which challenge non-German readers with tongue-twister length and complexity (see, for example, under Plate G3). It also makes choosing British Royal Navy equivalent ranks – e.g. in Table 5, in plate commentaries and photo captions – an even more approximate process than usual.

Naval rank classes

On 17 October 1936, Line rank titles were divided into seven classes or groups (*Hauptklassen*), as follows, from senior to junior:

(1) Flag officers (Großadmiral – Konteradmiral); (2) senior Line officers

(Kommodore – Korvettenkapitän); (3) Line commanders and lieutenants (Kapitänleutnant – Leutnant); (4) Band WOs (Marineobermusikinspizient – Marinemusikmeister, omitted from this study); (5) senior NCOs (Oberwaffenwart – Bootsmann); (6) junior NCOs (Oberbootsmannsmaat – Bootsmannsmaat); and (7) ratings (Matrosenoberstabsgefreiter – Matrose).

TABLE 6: Selective navy-blue uniform branch badges and titles, 21 May 1935–8 May 1945

1. Officers: Cuff; silver/ gold shoulder strap branch badge *Most senior rank-title in branch*	2. Senior NCOs: Gold shoulder strap branch badge *Feldwebel-equivalent rank-title*	3. Junior NCOs and ratings: Gold sleeve branch badge (NCOs, with anchor). *Gefreiter/ Matrose rank-titles*
1. Line officers: gold cuff star; no strap badge e.g. *Großadmiral*	**1.** Boatswain: fouled anchor *Bootsmann*	**1.** Boatswain: gold star *Matrosengefreiter / Matrose*
1. Line officers: gold cuff star, no strap badge e.g. *Admiral*	**2.** Navigation: crossed anchors *Steuermann*	**2.** Navigation: sextant *Steuermannsgefreiter / Matrose*
1. Line officers: gold cuff star, no strap badge e.g. *Kapitän zur See*	**3.** Survey: crossed anchors, sextant *Vermessungssteuermann*	**3.** Survey: sextant *Vermessungsgefreiter / Matrose*
2. General Service officers; gold cuff star, no strap badge e.g. *Kapitän zur See (des Allgemeinen Marinedienstes – AMD)*	**4.** General Service: anchor *Feldwebel*	**4.** General Service: anchor *Gefreiter / Matrose*
3. Naval Artillery officers: winged shell on cuff/ & strap e.g. *Kapitän zur See (der Marineartillerie – MA)*	**5.** Naval Artillery: anchor, winged shell *Marineartilleriefeldwebel*	**5.** Naval Artillery: winged shell *Marineartilleriegefreiter / Marineartillerist*
4. Engineer officers; cogwheel on cuff & strap e.g. *Admiral (des Ingenieurwesens - Ing)*	**6.** Engineers: anchor, cogwheel *Maschinist*	**6.** Engineers: cogwheel *Maschinistengefreiter / Matrose*
5. Weapons Systems officers: crossed cannons on cuff & strap e.g. *Konteradmiral (des Waffenwesens - W)*	**7.** Artillery Engineers: anchor, crossed cannons, chevron *Oberwaffenwart*	**7.** Artillery Engineers: cogwheel, crossed cannons *Mechanikergefreiter / Matrose*
6. Barrage weapons officers; mine on cuff & strap e.g. *Konteradmiral (des Waffenwesens – W)*	**8.** Barrage machinists: anchor, mine, chevron *Oberwaffenwart*	**8.** Barrage machinists: cogwheel, mine *Mechanikergefreiter / Matrose*
7. Torpedo technical officers: torpedo, cogwheel on cuff & strap e.g. *Kapitän zur See (des technischen Torpedowesens – T)*	**9.** Torpedo technicians: anchor, cogwheel, torpedo *Mechaniker*	**9.** Torpedo technicians: cogwheel, torpedo *Mechanikergefreiter / Matrose*
1. Line officers: gold cuff star, no strap badge e.g. *Kapitän zur See*	**10.** Artificers: anchor, crossed cannons *Feuerwerker*	**10.** Artificers: crossed cannons *Feuerwerksgefreiter / Matrose*
1. Line officers: gold cuff star, no strap badge e.g. *Kapitän zur See*	**11.** Signals: anchor, crossed flags *Signalmeister*	**11.** Signals; crossed flags *Signalgefreiter / Matrose*
8. Signals officers: lightning bolt on cuff & strap e.g. *Kapitän zur See (des Nachrichtenwesens - MN)*	**12.** Telephones: anchor, six crossed arrows *Fernschreibmeister*	**12.** Telephones: 6 crossed arrows *Fernschreibgefreiter / Matrose.*
8. Signals officers: lightning bolt on cuff & strap e.g. *Kapitän zur See (des Nachrichtenwesens – MN)*	**13.** Radar: anchor, 2 horizontal lightning bolts *Funkmeister*	**13.** Radar: 2 horizontal lightning bolts *Funkgefreiter / Matrose*
1. Line officers: gold star on cuff, no strap badge e.g. *Kapitän zur See*	**14.** Air Raid Warning: wing, anchor, crossed lightning flashes *Flugmeldefeldwebel*	**14.** Air Raid Warning: wing, anchor, crossed lightning flashes *Flugmeldegefreiter / Flugmelder*
9. Administration officers: Mercury Staff on cuff & strap e.g. *Konteradmiral (der Marineverwaltung – V)*	**15.** Administration: anchor, Mercury staff *Verwaltungsfeldwebel*	**15.** Administration: Mercury Staff; *Verwaltungsgefreiter / Matrose*
9. Administration officers (TSD): Mercury staff above bar on cuff/strap; e.g. *Admiraloberstabsintendant*	–	–
1. Line officers: gold star on cuff, no strap badge e.g. *Kapitän zur See*	**16.** Clerks: crossed quills on anchor *Schreiberfeldwebel*	**16.** Clerks: crossed quills *Schreibergefreiter / Matrose*
10. Judge Advocate officers (TSD); sword above bar on cuff/ strap e.g. *Admiraloberstabsrichter*	–	–
11. Medical officers: Aesculapius staff on cuff & strap e.g. *Admiraloberstabsarzt*	**17.** Medical staff: anchor, Aesculapius staff *Sanitätsfeldwebel*	**17.** Medical staff: *Sanitätsgefreiter / Matrose*
1. Line officers: gold cuff star, no strap badge *Kapitän zur See*	**18.** Motor Transport: steering wheel on anchor *Kraftfahrfeldwebel*	**18.** Motor Transport: steering wheel *Kraftfahrgefreiter / Kraftfahrer*

Explanatory note:
Please note that, for readers' convenience, the author has added numbers for the branches selected; these *do not correspond* with official German numbering. For ease, read down Column 2 to desired branch, then check left and right to match with officers and junior ranks.

Insignia on navy-blue uniforms

Officers wore rank insignia on the cuffs of the navy-blue service tunic, comprising a gold-wire branch-badge above gold-braid rings: wide (5.2cm) for flag officers, medium (1.6cm) for most officers, alternating with narrow (0.9cm) for *Fregattenkapitän* and *Kapitänleutnant*.

On the greatcoat, flag officers wore shoulder straps of interwoven cords (one silver, and two gold or later gold-yellow celleon) on, for all officer ranks, navy-blue underlay. Their straps bore aluminium 4-point rank stars, and some a branch badge (omitted for all Line officers). Senior officers wore plaited double aluminium-cord shoulder straps with gilt metal rank stars and (if non-Line) branch badges. Junior officers wore flat aluminium-cord straps with the same type of insignia.

On the service tunic and greatcoat, senior NCOs wore flat, stiff, navy-blue shoulder boards with a pointed inner end, with silver metal 4-point stars and a gold metal branch-badge (Line NCOs, a fouled anchor and a gold metal chevron). On the upper left sleeve of the parade jacket and pea-jacket junior NCOs wore a navy-blue cloth oval bearing a gold metal or yellow thread branch badge of an unfouled anchor, with a small point-down seniority chevron. Junior NCOs also initially wore 1–2 silver braid bars across mid-blue cloth collar patches on the pea-jacket, but from 1 Dec 1939 these were replaced with cornflower-blue patches with 1–2 gold braids, plus braid collar edging. On the sailors' jumper, parade jacket and pea-jacket, ratings wore a yellow-thread branch badge on the left upper sleeve, above yellow thread or cut-out cloth full-size rank chevrons (from senior to junior: two or one chevrons enclosing four-point star; three, two or one chevrons).

Insignia on white uniforms

Officers and senior NCOs wore 'greatcoat' shoulder straps on the White Tropical Service Dress and White Landing Dress. On the jumpers of White Fatigue Dress and White Landing Dress, junior NCOs wore their sleeve insignia in cornflower-blue on white cloth; on the White Landing Dress jumper ratings wore the yellow-on-navy-blue branch badge and chevrons, but cornflower-blue 4-point rank stars on white.

Insignia on brown and grey work uniforms

Officers and senior NCOs wore shoulder straps of rank on the brown Barracks Service Dress, grey Fatigue Dress, and grey or brown Submarine Fatigues. Junior NCOs might wear white-metal 'chevrons' on the collar point in imitation of the collar braid of their rank group, but ratings wore no rank insignia.

Insignia on brown tropical uniforms

On the shoulder straps of the tropical shirt and service dress tunic, officers wore 'greatcoat' rank insignia in matt-grey on brown underlay. Senior NCOs wore pointed brown shoulder straps with silver metal 4-point stars and dark blue ribbon edging. Junior NCOs had the same (*Oberbootsmannsmaat*), or without ribbon edging across the base (*Bootsmannsmaat*). Ratings wore dark blue rank stars and chevrons on the sleeve.

Insignia on field-grey uniforms

Officers wore 'greatcoat' rank shoulder straps on the field tunic and greatcoat. Senior NCOs had yellow NCO braid around the tunic collar; their pointed dark green (field-grey from 1940) shoulder-straps had NCO-

BELOW LEFT
Naval personnel in port listen to the radio. They are wearing tropical brown M1939 sun-helmets with M1941 shirts and shorts, though one retains his navy-blue on-board cap. (Bundesarchiv Bild 146-1994-003-16, Matrosen beim Radio hören.jpg)

BELOW RIGHT
Portrait of a Naval Artillery rating, taken 22 May 1943. His M1942 field tunic is all field-grey, including the painted buttons, and the Navy's distinctive pointed shoulder straps (whose yellow-thread branch badge is not visible here, but would have been a flaming shell superimposed on a vertical anchor). The M1943 standard grey collar *Litzen* have a light grey (replacing white) central separation stripe. He seems to have privately acquired a silver-wire breast eagle on dark green backing. (Courtesy Christopher Harrod Collection)

RIGHT

Oberleutnant (MA) Walter Ohmsen commanded a battery of 260th Naval Artillery Bn at Crisbecq, covering 'Utah Beach' in Normandy; this claimed to be the first battery to engage the Allied landing force on 6 June 1944. Wounded during five days' heavy fighting, Ohmsen broke through to the new German lines on 11 June; for his bravery he was awarded both classes of the Iron Cross and the Knight's Cross, all of which he displays here. His field-grey *Feldmütze* has officers' silver flap-piping, a light grey eagle-and-swastika, and a tricolour cockade on diamond-shaped backing. His M1935 tunic bears dark green collar patches with silver *Litzen* with yellow centre-stripes and a white separation. His breast eagle is light grey machine-woven on field-grey. Here his silver-cord shoulder straps on navy-blue underlay show the second gold 4-point star of his promotion to *Kapitänleutnant,* equivalent to an Army *Hauptmann.* (Bundesarchiv_ Bild_183-R638498, Walter Ohmsen.jpg / Wikimedia Commons)

FAR RIGHT

The band insignia of the officers' peaked cap was 'three-dimensional', being worked on a navy-blue pad. This portrait photo shows the single gold-embroidered oakleaf peak edging of ranks from *Korvettenkapitän* up to *Kapitän zur See*. The subject is *Fregattenkapitän* Wolfgang Lüth, Germany's second-ranking submarine ace, who sank 46 ships during 15 patrols. He earned the Knight's Cross with Oakleaves, Swords and Diamonds, and the U-Boat War Badge with Diamonds; here he wears the Oakleaves, awarded on 13 Nov 1943. Lüth survived the war, but only by a week: when returning drunk to his quarters on the night of 13/14 May 1945 he was mistakenly shot by a German sentry. (Wolfgang Lüth.png / Wikimedia Commons)

braid edging, and silver metal 4-point rank stars. Junior NCOs had yellow NCO-braid edging on the shoulder straps: on all edges for *Obermaat*, but not across the base for *Maat*. Ratings had a yellow braid 4-point star and/ or chevrons on the left upper sleeve on dark green triangular backing (field-grey from 1940).

Naval Engineer Construction Battalion officers used Army rank titles and black Army Engineer underlay, but wore Navy 'greatcoat' rank insignia on the shoulder straps of the field tunic and greatcoat. NCOs wore field-grey round-ended shoulder straps piped black outside silver braid edging (mouse-grey from 1940), which for *Unteroffiziere* did not cross the base, and silver metal 4-point rank stars. Privates had rounded field-grey shoulder straps with black piping; their left sleeves bore silver-grey point-down chevrons with 4-point stars where appropriate, on a field-grey triangular backing. The Naval Fortress Engineer corps wore Army shoulder-straps with black officers' underlay (red for general officers). NCOs had yellow braid edgings, and privates' yellow braid sleeve chevrons.

BRANCH INSIGNIA

(See also Tables 6 & 7, pages 51 & 55)
As a highly technical service the Navy comprised a large (and steadily evolving) number of branches, designated 'careers' (*Laufbahnen*). The insignia of a selection of the most important branches are indicated in Tables 6 and 7.

Officers' branch insignia
Officers wore gold-wire branch badges above the cuff rank rings on the service tunic, and gold metal versions on the greatcoat shoulder straps (except by Line officers). There were 18 officer branches, of which the 11 most important are listed in Table 6. Line officers formed the most numerous branch, providing the 'seaman' or 'watch' officers aboard ship, and also the commissioned ranks in a number of other branches; the crucially important

Branch (Highest rank)	Gold/ yellow shoulder-strap branch insignia	Updated gold/ yellow shoulder-strap branch insignia
TABLE 7: Selective Land Forces navy-blue & field-grey uniform branch badges, pre- and post-March 1939		
Section A. Navy-blue and field-grey uniforms		
1. Naval Artillery (*Admiral (MA)*)	Roman Bn number above two crossed anchors (1935); Arabic Bn number above two crossed anchors (early 1939)	Arabic Bn number above flaming winged shell on vertical anchor (13 Mar 1939)
2. Engineer Officers, Naval Artillery (*Konteradmiral (Ing)*)	Cogwheel	–
3. Weapons Systems Officers, Naval Artillery (*Konteradmiral (W)*)	Crossed cannons	–
4. Naval Depot units (*Admiral*)	'N / O' above two crossed anchors (until 13 Mar 1939)	Two crossed anchors (13 Mar 1939)
5. Medical Service (*Admiralarzt*)	Snake and Aesculapius staff	–
Section B. Navy field-grey uniform		
6. Naval Infantry (*Konteradmiral / Generalmajor*) April 1940/ Feb 1945	–	–
7. Naval NCO Training Bns (*Kapitän zur See*)	two crossed anchors (until 13 Mar 1939)	Arabic Bn number above fouled anchor (13 Mar 1939)
8. Naval Special Bn (*Kapitän zur See*)	two crossed anchors (9 Nov 1936)	'S' above two crossed anchors (Wartime Special Bn, Sept 1939)
9. Naval AA Artillery (*Kapitän zur See*)	Arabic Bn number above flaming winged shell on vertical anchor (26 Aug 1939)	–
10. Naval Signals (*Kapitän zur See*)	(None)	–
11. Naval Radar Bns (*Korvettenkapitän*)	(None)	–
12. Air Warning Service (*Kapitän zur See*)	Arabic Bn number over wing, on four lightning bolts, above two crossed anchors (9 Apr 1938)	–
13. Motorized Transport units (*Korvettenkapitän*)	Steering wheel on vertical anchor	
Section C. Army field-grey uniform		
14. Naval Construction Bns (*Oberstleutnant*)	Black piping and shoulder-strap underlay	–
15. Naval Fortress Engineer Bns (*Generalmajor (MPi)*)	Black piping and shoulder-strap underlay	

Engineer and Weapons System officers were fewer in number. Most officers held traditional Navy ranks (e.g. *Kapitän zur See* down to *Leutnant zur See*) with few non-Line officers reaching flag rank. Table 6 Column 1 shows the highest officer rank possible in each branch. Non-Line titles were usually followed by an identifying suffix (e.g. *Ing* for *Ingenieur*). All captains used the *zur See* suffix, but this was omitted in non-Line branches for *Oberleutant*, *Leutnant*, *Oberfähnrich* and *Fähnrich* titles, while Medical and Dental officers retained their traditional '*Arzt / Zahnarzt*' titles. On 24 Jan 1944 administrative and legal Naval Officials were redesignated officers of the 'Troop Special Service' (*Truppensonderdienst* – TSD), with *Intendant* ('administrator') and *Richter* ('judge advocate') ranks clearly inspired by those of the Medical Service.

Senior NCOs' branch insignia

Senior NCOs wore a gold metal branch badge superimposed on an unfouled anchor (*Bootsmänner* only, fouled anchor) on the shoulder straps of navy-blue service tunics and greatcoats. Branch insignia were not worn on the shoulder straps of brown tropical service tunics, shirts or accompanying field-grey greatcoats. With effect from 1 Apr 1938 the senior NCOs' designations were

Two leading seamen/ junior NCOs (*Maate*) wearing navy-blue service dress with the pea-jacket. Both have the yellow machine-woven breast eagle; a single gold braid rank bar on the cornflower-blue collar patches; and the gold braid collar-edging of this rank group. The man on the left has the buttonhole ribbon of the Iron Cross 2nd Class; his comrade has just been awarded it, and for today only wears the cross on its suspension ribbon. (Bundesarchiv N 1603 Bild-037, Rumänien, Marine-Filberichter G / Wikimedia Commons)

reorganized into 41 branch variations, numbered I–XVIII with suffix letters denoting sub-branches. For simplicity, in Table 6 the author has reduced these to a selection of 18 of the most important branches. Each branch had its own range of non-commissioned rank titles, each initially made up from a regular rank-prefix (*Oberstabs-, Ober-*), then a branch-specific title, then a rank-suffix (*-feldwebel, -meister*). From 31 Jan 1938 all branch indicators were placed first in the word: thus *Sanitätstabsoberfeldwebel* instead of *Obersanitätsfeldwebel*. (On the same date *Oberfernschreibfeldwebel* was changed to *Oberfernschreibmeister*, simply because the latter sounded better.) Table 6, Column 2 gives examples of the *Bootsmann*-equivalent branch rank titles.

Junior NCOs' branch insignia

Junior NCOs wore the same branch badges as senior NCOs, but in yellow thread or private-purchase gold metal on a navy-blue cloth oval on the left upper sleeve of the navy-blue jumper, pea-jacket and parade jacket, and in blue thread on a white cloth oval on white jumpers. Branch insignia were not worn (at least officially) on the brown tropical tunic or shirt, nor on the brown barracks service dress, or on grey or brown fatigues. Junior NCOs were enrolled in the same branches as senior NCOs (with the exception of *Oberwaffenwart* and *Waffenwart*). They bore rank-titles including the elements *-obermaat / -maat/*, or *-fedwebel/ -meister* (e.g. *Obersanitätsmaat/ Sanitätsfeldwebel*; *Oberfunkmaat/ Funkmeister*, etc.).

Ratings' branch insignia

Ratings wore the yellow-thread junior NCOs' branch badge without the anchor, on a navy-blue cloth circle on the left upper sleeve of the same garments as above, just touching the navy-blue cloth backing of the chevrons in the case of senior ratings. Again, it was made in blue-on-white for white clothing, but was not worn on brown uniforms or on grey or brown fatigues. Ratings' branches were the same as for NCOs, the most important 18 branches being listed in Table 6, Column 3. Before 1 Apr 1938 the rank-titles were composed of the branch-title followed by a rank. The word *Gast* (literally, 'guest') was used for the lowest ranks (e.g. for Engineers, *Maschinistengast*, *Obermaschinistengast* and then *Maschinistengefreiter*, etc.) From 1 Apr 1938 ratings' ranks were updated and simplified, with the most junior seamen designated as *Matrosen*, as shown in Table 6, Column 3 (e.g. *Matrose*, then *Maschinistengefreiter* and *Maschinistenobergefreiter*, etc.).

Land forces branch insignia
(See also Table 7, page 55)

Branches listed in Table 7, Section A (numbered 1–5) wore field-grey uniforms when operational on land, and navy-blue uniforms when deployed aboard ship or on office duties. Badges included that of the most important land branch, the Naval Artillery, and its Engineering and Weapons Systems supporting units, but also Depot units and the Medical service. Table 7, Section B lists eight land branches (numbered 6–13), which wore exclusively

BELOW LEFT
The service branch of this Medical senior leading seaman (*Sanitätsobermaat*) is identified by the yellow-thread badge on navy-blue oval backing sewn to the upper left sleeve of his pea-jacket. It shows an anchor crossed with the 'staff of Aesculapius' above a small seniority chevron. (Courtesy Christopher Harrod Collection)

BELOW RIGHT
France, 1942: an Administration-branch leading seaman at his desk aboard a warship. His branch badge is a winged 'Mercury staff' with two entwined snakes, superimposed on a vertical anchor, all worked in yellow thread on a navy-blue oval. Note that those entitled to campaign shields (in this case that for the 1940 Narvik campaign) wore them on the left sleeve above all other badges. (Bundesarchiv Bild 101II-MW-5942-23. Frankreich, Dienst an Bord / Wikimedia Commons)

the M1935 Navy version of the German Army field-grey M1935 field uniform. These included the Naval Infantry, which had formed *ad hoc* units from June 1940, but were greatly expanded in Feb 1945. Section C shows only Army Construction and Fortress Engineer Battalions, transferred to the Navy in 1942 still wearing Army uniforms and insignia.

Flag officers wore gold-and-silver interwoven-cord shoulder straps with navy-blue underlay on navy-blue uniforms, or dark green underlay with field-grey uniforms (red for generals of Fortress Engineers). The only branch badges worn were those of Engineer officers (silver cogwheel), Weapons Systems officers (silver crossed cannons), and the Medical Service (silver snake and Aesculapius staff).

Senior and junior officers wore silver-wire or matt-grey plaited and flat cord shoulder straps respectively, with navy-blue underlay on navy-blue uniforms or dark green underlay on field-grey uniforms (black underlay for Construction and Fortress Engineers). Engineer, Weapons Systems and Medical officers wore the same branch badges as flag officers, but in gold metal.

Senior and junior NCOs wore M1935 dark green (1940, field-grey) pointed shoulder straps with yellow braid edging, and gold metal Roman or Arabic unit numbers above gold metal branch badges. Ratings wore the same minus the braid edgings, and on the upper left sleeve yellow braid chevrons with 4-point stars as appropriate. Some branches (see Table 7, Sections B and C) had their Roman battalion numbers changed to Arabic numbers in early 1939, but on 13 Mar 1939 the numbers were abolished altogether for security reasons. Some branches also changed their branch badge, usually to a pattern incorporating crossed unfouled anchors. Naval Construction and Fortress Engineer battalions wore Army black piping, with silver/ matt grey or yellow braid NCO edgings and ratings' chevrons, respectively, but no branch badges.

GERMANY, 1945

(H1) *Konteradmiral* (*Ing*); Hamburg, February 1945

This rear admiral of Engineers is wearing the flag officers' field-grey service uniform according to regulations of 26 May 1943. Even for generals' rank the peaked cap has dark green piping, matching the colour of the band. The insignia and chin cords are of gold wire, and the peak is plain black. The M1935 tunic has gold 'anchor' buttons, and a gold-wire breast eagle; the patches on the dark-green collar are cornflower-blue, bearing M1900 gold-wire *Larisch* embroidery. His flag officers' shoulder straps on dark green underlay are of interwoven gold/ silver cord, with a silver cogwheel Engineer branch badge. His field-grey riding breeches have cornflower-blue *Lampassen* – seam-piping between two stripes. As well as both classes of the Iron Cross, he displays (on his right breast) the superior award of the German Cross.

(H2) *Leutnant* (*MA*), 1st Naval Infantry Division; Prenzlau, April 1945

This lieutenant of Naval Artillery probably commands the remnant of a battery fighting as infantry in the 'last ditch' behind the collapsing Oder front south of Stettin. He wears conventional field uniform under an M1935 officers' greatcoat with gold 'anchor' buttons. The peaked service cap has gold insignia but silver chin cords, and the usual dark green band and piping. The flat light grey cord shoulder straps of a *Leutnant*,

here on dark green underlay, bear no rank star, but show the gold flaming-shell-and-anchor *Marineartillerie* branch badge. Under his greatcoat the dark green collar of his tunic is just visible, with its silver, yellow and white *Litzen* on dark green patches. On the brown leather service belt he has attached two triple magazine pouches for the 9mm MP40 sub-machinegun.

(H3) *Matrosenobergefreiter*, 2nd Naval Infantry Division; Rethem, April 1945

The defence of Rethem against British 53rd (Welsh) Inf Div on 11/12 April saw elements of 5. Marine-Grenadier Rgt putting up one of this division's typically determined fights. This senior able seaman apparently combines the roles of squad leader and 'first gunner' of an MG42 team, presumably as a result of heavy casualties. He wears the field-grey M1943 field cap, and his cap insignia and sleeve rank chevrons are as in Plate G1. He wears the all-field-grey M1940 tunic; the collar *Litzen*, all in shades of grey, are factory-attached directly to the collar. The pointed shoulder-straps bear the yellow-thread M1939 Depot Bn branch badge of crossed unfouled anchors. His trousers are confined by greenish-grey webbing 'retreat anklets' (in fact introduced for economy as early as 8 Aug 1940), above black leather ankle boots. His belt equipment, with a Navy buckle, includes a holstered pistol for self-defence, and the MG spares pouch at his right front. His MG42 is fitted with a 50-round belt-drum.

OTHER INSIGNIA

TRADE BADGES

From 1933, junior NCOs and ratings displayed trade badges marking successful completion of specialist training. These were worn on the left arm below any rank insignia, and ratings could wear up to two badges at a time. Worked on navy-blue, white, dark-green or field-grey cloth patches as appropriate, they comprised red woollen, cotton or artificial-silk thread images, above, where appropriate, 1–3 small red point-down seniority chevrons for advanced qualifications or long service. In all, 31 different badges were in use 1933–40, superseded by a revised system 9 Aug 1940–48 May 1945. The list is too long and complex to allow a systematic description here; there were, for example, 14 different qualifications for a gun captain (*Geschützführer*), all based on the flaming shell motif.[5]

WAR BADGES

Up to two of seven pinback metal badges might be worn on the left lower breast. They were awarded according to various calculations of criteria involving time served at sea, numbers of combat actions, wounds in action, survival of own ships being sunk or acts of bravery not judged worthy of the Iron Cross 2nd Class. An eighth was the Naval Artillery War Badge for land service, with its own complicated points-based criteria. For all badges, the bureaucratic requirements might simply be waived by commanding officers to acknowledge particularly meritorious service.

Submarine War Badge, reinstated 13 Oct 1939 for submarine combat service. Gold submarine in horizontal oval oakleaf wreath, topped by spread eagle with black swastika. From 1941 onward, 29 U-boat 'aces' (five sinkings) already holding the Knight's Cross with Oakleaves received this badge upgraded to silver gilt with a silver swastika bearing eight diamonds.

Most other war badges showed vertical oval wreaths:

Destroyer War badge, instituted 4 June 1940 for combat service on destroyers, and also torpedo boats and speed boats. Angled grey destroyer bow making bow-wave, emerging to left from gold wreath topped with folded-wing eagle-and-swastika.

Minesweeper, Submarine-Hunter and Security War Badge, instituted 31 Aug 1940, for crews with basically protective/ escort duties. Silver explosion rising from sea, in gold wreath topped with spread eagle-and-swastika.

Blockade-Runner War Badge, instituted 1 Apr 1941 for personnel of the Merchant Navy, and of the *Kriegsmarine* assigned to merchant ships, for reaching port through an Allied blockade. Silver flying eagle (badge otherwise all grey) on left-angled bow of approaching merchant ship, in circular wreath. (No eagle-and-swastika.)

Auxiliary Cruiser War Badge, instituted 24 Apr 1941, for crews of armed merchant ships operating against Allied supply lines. Gold Viking ship approaching, angled to left, on grey part-globe of the Earth, in gold wreath topped with spread eagle-and-swastika.

High Seas Fleet War Badge, instituted 30 Apr 1941 for service on ships-of-the-line, battleships and cruisers. Head-on grey battleship, in gold wreath topped with spread eagle-and-swastika.

---

5 A large number of trade badges are illustrated on Plates 24–25 of Guido Rosignoli's *Naval and Marine Badges and Insignia of World War II* (Blandford Press, 1980)

Speed Boat War Badge, instituted 30 May 1941 in place of previously awarded Destroyer badge. First pattern: angled silver boat on waves, emerging to left from gold wreath topped with spread eagle-and-swastika. Second pattern (Jan 1943): slightly redesigned boat (now grey) and waves.

Naval Artillery War Badge, instituted 24 June 1941 for service in coastal artillery and land-based AA units. Grey, shielded heavy gun, barrel slanting to top left, emerging from gold wreath topped with folded-wing eagle-and-swastika.

COMBAT CLASPS & BADGES

As in the other armed services, *Frontspangen* were subsequently awarded for prolonged or distinguished combat service. They were worn on the upper left breast, above any medal ribbons.

Submarine Combat Clasp, instituted 15 May 1944. The bronze clasp depicted a miniature version of the M1939 Submarine War Badge centred between two 'spread wings' of triple oakleaf sprays. Higher grade in silver instituted 24 Nov 1944.

Small Battle Units Combat Badges & Clasp. The badges were instituted 30 Nov 1944, to be worn by *Kampfverbände* personnel on the upper right sleeve above any other badges. For basic proficiency: navy-blue cloth disc bearing yellow-thread sawfish swimming to right. Above this, seven grades (*Stufen*) were regulated for bravery and achievements in action, but it is probable that Grade 4 was the highest actually awarded. Grade 1, for one action: sawfish within circle of rope tied at top with open reef-knot. Grade 2, for two actions: with added broadsword slanted up from bottom right to top left, 'behind' the central blue disc within the rope circle. Grade 3, for three actions: with two diagonally crossed swords. Grade 4, for four actions: with one vertical and two diagonal swords.

15 June 1942, St Nazaire, France: an unidentified German submarine returns to the base of *6.* or *7. U-Flottillen* after a patrol. The white spots just discernible on the left side of the crewmens' on-board caps are an unofficial boat or flotilla badge. German researchers have only managed to identify with certainty a small minority of these which were actually worn. However, 6th Flotilla boats are known to have adopted the stylized 'Viking longship prow' from U-404, and 7th Flotilla the 'snorting bull of Scapa Flow' from U-47. (Bundesarchiv Bild 101II-MW-6434-15, St Nazaire, U-Boot einlaufend. Jpg / Wikimedia Commons)

Above this grade, metal Clasps were to be awarded, for wear on the upper left breast (while the Grade 4 cloth badge was retained on the right sleeve). The clasp showed the sawfish swimming left, superimposed on 'wings' of tangled rope loops. For five and six actions, the clasp was to be bronze; for seven to nine actions, silver; and for ten or more actions, gold.

CAMPAIGN SHIELDS

Seven *Wehrmacht* campaign shields were officially or unofficially awarded to Naval personnel among others, and worn on navy-blue cloth backing on the left upper sleeve above all other badges. Qualified personnel might wear two shields one above the other, and three shields with one above two.

Narvik Shield, instituted 19 Aug 1940, for service during the Norwegian campaign, 9 Apr–9 June 1940; 3,661 shields were awarded. For Navy, gold metal: folded-wing eagle-and-swastika surmounting shield with top title 'NARVIK', above '19' and '40' divided by an Edelweiss, above crossed fouled anchor and aircraft propeller.

Cholm Shield, instituted 1 July 1942 for defenders of the Cholm pocket, 21 Jan–4 May 1942, including a Navy transport unit. White metal shield bearing folded-wing eagle grasping Iron Cross with centred swastika, above two-line title 'CHOLM/ 1942'.

Crimea Shield, instituted 25 July 1942 for personnel engaged 21 Sept 1941–25 July 1942. Bronze metal; spread eagle-and-swastika between '1941' and '1942', above map of Crimea inscribed 'KRIM'.

Kuban Shield, instituted 20 Sept 1943 for personnel engaged 1 Feb–9 Oct 1943. Bronze metal; spread eagle-and-swastika between '19' and '43', above title 'KUBAN', above stylized map of Kuban bridgehead with dagged 'front line'.

(Unofficial) Lorient Shield, locally instituted Dec 1944 for defenders of besieged inactive U-boat base, 12 Aug 1944–10 May 1945. Tall, narrow shield, crudely made in white or yellow metal; '19' and '44' flanking head of naked warrior with helmet, sword and shield bearing small eagle-and-swastika, bestriding defences.

(Unofficial) Dunkirk cap shield, locally instituted Dec 1944 for wear on left side of peaked or on-board caps by defenders of the besieged port, 15 Sept 1944–9 May 1945. Described as crudely made of thin stamped yellow metal, *c.*34mm wide by 41mm tall; title 'DUENKIRCHEN', above Dunkirk lighthouse tower flanked by '19' and '44', above waves, above a chain.

(Unofficial) Lappland Shield, locally instituted Feb 1945 for personnel fighting there since Sept 1944, but issued only after 9 May 1945. Usually white metal; folded-wing eagle-and-swastika, above title 'LAPPLAND', above map of northern Finnish coast.

CUFF TITLES

During the Third Reich, formations and units of the *Wehrmacht* and a range of paramilitary and National Socialist political organizations were authorized a wide range of cuff titles. These were usually machine-woven, 3.2cm (1.26 ins) wide with an edging. They extended right around the left or right forearm above the cuff until 18 Nov 1944, when they were restricted to 25cm (9.84 ins) long to be attached only around the outer, front and back surfaces of the sleeve. *Kriegsmarine* personnel were officially eligible for only four such titles, of which only one was exclusive to the Navy:

Africa Corps, Army pattern, authorized 18 July 1941 for two months' service in the Corps; extended on 4 Nov 1941 to all Panzer Group Africa personnel. It bore a white or aluminium-wire title 'AFRIKAKORPS' on a dark green cloth band with white or aluminium inner borders and light tan-brown outer borders, worn on the right sleeve. From Dec 1942 some naval personnel unofficially adopted a navy-blue band with a gold machine-woven 'AFRIKAKORPS' or 'AFRIKA' title and edgings.

Crete, authorized 16 Oct 1942 for personnel who fought during the capture of the island 20–27 May 1942. A white linen band 3.3cm (1.3 ins) wide had machine-embroidered gold-yellow edging and the title 'KRETA' flanked by acanthus leaves, to be worn on the left sleeve.

Africa and Palm Trees. The Army pattern, authorized 15 Jan 1943 for six months' service in North Africa or for wounds, and worn on the left sleeve. The 'donkey'–brown fine wool band bore in silver-grey cotton thread the title 'AFRIKA' flanked by two palm-tree heads, with matching edgings. Some Navy personnel unofficially adopted a navy-blue band with gold-wire 'AFRIKA' and palm-tree heads, with or without gold edgings.

Hitler Youth. The only exclusively naval pattern, authorized in Oct 1944 for the Navy Special Forces 1st Assault Boat Flotilla, which was entirely composed of former HJ members. The navy-blue band bore the yellow machine-woven title '*Hitlerjugend*' and matching edgings.

Some Navy personnel are known to have worn non-Navy cuffbands, such as the black on grey-white 'KURLAND' title locally made in Courland (now Kurzeme, NW Latvia) for service there during 9 Oct 1944–10 May 1945.

INDEX

Page numbers in **bold** refer to illustrations and those in *italic* denote tables.

Admiral Graf Spee 20, **49**
Admiral Hipper 18–19, 20–21, 30
Admiral Scheer 20
aircraft 30–31, **30**
anti-mine, anti-submarine, patrol and security vessels 26, 28–29
  battle order *24*
Aviso '*Grille*' 7 (6)

badges *see* insignia and badges
Bartels, *KL*. Hans 14
Bismarck 6, 9, 18, 21
Blücher 20, 21

campaign shields *see* insignia and badges
campaigns
  Spain 1936–39: 4
  surface operations 1939–45: 4–10
capital ships
  aircraft carrier 18, 20
  battleships 18–20
  pocket battleships 20
casualties and losses 10, 31
'Channel Dash' 1942 6, 8, 19, 21
convoys 8–9, 10
cruisers
  auxiliary cruisers 22, 24, 60
  heavy cruisers 20–21
  light cruisers 21–22

destroyers 22, 60
Deutschland 20
Dönitz, *Großadmiral* Karl 4, 9, 10, 11, 12, 14, 33 (32)

Emden 21
escort boats 29

foreign volunteers
  Croatian Naval Legion 37, 39 (38), 41
  guard units 42
  Spain 33 (32), 41
France 5–6, 10, 11–12

German Minesweeping Administration 12–13
Gneisenau 6, 18, 19–20
Graf Spee 4–5
Graf Zeppelin 18, 20

Hansa 22, 24
Hitler, Adolf 4, 5, 8–9, 12
Hood, HMS 6, 9, 18, 21

insignia and badges 4 (5), 7 (6), 15 (14), 23 (22), 27 (26), 39 (38), 43, 48, 50
  (Unofficial) Dunkirk Cap Shield 62
  (Unofficial) Lappland Shield 62
  (Unofficial) Lorient Shield 62
  administration branch 57
  admiral 59 (58)
  Africa and Palm Trees cuff title 63
  Africa Corps cuff title 23 (22), 63
  artillery units 54
  Auxiliary Cruiser War Badge 60
  Blockade-Runner War Badge 13, 60
  branch badges and titles navy-blue uniforms *51*
  brown and grey work uniforms 53
  brown tropical uniforms 53, *53*
  campaign shields 57, 62
  Cholm Shield 62
  combat clasps and badges 61–62
  Crete cuff title 63
  Crimea Shield 37, 62
  cuff titles 7 (6), 8, 62–63
  Destroyer War Badge 60
  engineer units 54
  field grey uniforms 53–54, **53**, 54, *55*, 59 (58)
  High Seas Fleet War Badge 60
  Hitler Youth cuff title 63
  junior NCOs' branch insignia 56, **56**
  Kuban Shield 62
  land forces *55*, 57–58
  line rank insignia 45–46
  M1936 Pilots' Badge 39 (38)
  medical services 57, 58
  Minesweeper, Submarine-Hunter and Security War Badges 13, 43, 60
  Narvik Shield 15 (14), 44, 57, 62

Naval Artillery War Badge 15 (14), 60, 61
navy-blue uniforms *51*, 52, **52**, *55*, **56**
  officers' branch insignia 54–55
  ratings' branch insignia 57
  senior NCOs' branch insignia 55–56
Small Battle Units Combat Badges and Clasps 61–62
Speed Boat War Badge 61
Submarine Combat Clasp 61
Submarine War Badge 27 (26), 60, 61
trade badges 60
unofficial badges **61**
war badges 60–61
white uniforms 53
intelligence 10
Italy 5, 6, 9, 11

Japan 11

Karlsruhe 21
Köln 21
Königsberg 21
Kretschmer, *Kapitänleutnant* Otto **12**

land forces
  air warning service 40, 49 (48)
  artillery 36–37, 39 (38), 53
  battle order *40*
  depot units 35
  engineer units 38, 49 (48), 50, 54
  guard units 41, 42
  infantry 32, 34–35, 59 (58)
  motor transport units 40–41
  naval replacement units 35–36
  NCO training units 36
  penal units 35
  signals units 38, 40
  uniforms 44, 49 (48)
Langsdorff, *Kapitän zur See* Hans 4–5
Luftwaffe 30–31
Lüth, *Fregattenkapitän* Wolfgang 54
Lütjens, *Vizeadmiral* Günther 42
Lützow 20, 21

Malta 6
Marschall, Wilhelm 17
medals and awards 4 (5), 7 (6), 8, 14, 17, 54, 56, 59 (58)
Mediterranean campaign 6, 23 (22)
merchant navy 13–14
minesweepers 26, 43
  auxiliary minesweepers 28
  clearance minesweepers 26, 28
  war badges 13, **43**, 60

naval aviation 30–31, **30**
naval lineage 5
naval organization
  North Sea & Baltic Sea 'Stations'/Naval Group Commands 14, 16
  regional organization 16–17
North Cape, Battle of the 19
Norway 5, 21

Ohmsen, *Oberleutnant* Walter 54
Operation 'Hannibal' 9, 17, 21
Operation 'Weserübung' 5

patrol and security boats 28–29
Prien, *Kl*. Gunther **12**
Prinz Eugen 6, 21–22

radar 10
Raeder, *Generaladmiral* Erich 4, 5, 6, 9, 12, 14, 16
ranks
  insignia *45–46*
  naval rank classes *50–51*
River Plate, Battle of the 4–5, **49**
Royal Navy 4–5, 18
Ruge, *Kommodore* Friedrich-Oskar **43**

Scharnhorst 6, 18–19, 20
Schlesien 17
Schleswig-Holstein 4, 17
Schmundt, *Konteradmiral* Hubert 8
Seydlitz 21
Spanish Civil War 4, 34
special forces 30
speed boats 19, 25–26, 61
submarine-hunters 29, 60
submarine operations 10–12, **12**, **13**, 20, 28, 61

battle order *21*
combat clasps 61
Submarine War Badge 60
U-boats 29–31
uniforms 27 (26), 48
surface ships
  battle order *18*
  ships-of-the-line 17

Tirpitz 6, 9, 18
Topp, *Kapitänleutnant* Erich 28
torpedo boats 25
training 35, 36
Tripartite Pact 11

U-109 20
U-123 **13**
uniforms
  admiral 33 (32), 42, 59 (58)
  artillery units 35, 53, 54, 59 (58)
  Atlantic & Baltic 1943–45 33 (32)
  Atlantic Front, 1941–43: 15 (14)
  belt equipment 49, 59 (58)
  Black Sea & English Channel, 1942–43: 39 (38)
  Bootsmann 33 (32)
  brown uniforms 22 (21), 27 (26), 44, 46, 48, 50, 53
  caps 4 (5), 7 (6), **10**, **12**, 15 (14), 22 (21), 27 (26), 39 (38), 43, 44, 47 (46), 49–50, 49, 52, 53, 54, 59 (58)
  captured uniforms **12**, 28, 48
  ceremonial dress 16, 43
  Croatian Naval Legion 37, 39 (38)
  fatigue uniforms 48, 53
  Flugmeldeobergefreiter, air warning bns 44
  Fregattenkapitän 7 (6)
  full dress 42
  Funkmaat 23 (22)
  Gefreiter 33 (32)
  German Minesweeping Administration 13, **14**
  grey uniforms 33 (32), 35, 39 (38), 47 (46), 49–50, 53–54, **53**, 54, *55*, 59 (58)
  Hauptfeldwebel 7 (6)
  helmets 48, 53
  Kapitän sur Zee 17
  Kapitänleutnant (submarines) 27 (26)
  Korvettenkapitän 23 (22)
  land forces 44, 49 (48), *55*
  landing dress 15 (14), 39 (38), 44, 53
  Marineartilleriefeldwebel 15 (14)
  Marinefestungspioniersstabsoberfeldwebel 49 (48)
  Mediterranean campaign, 1942: 23 (22)
  merchant navy 13–14
  navy-blue uniforms 7 (6), 15 (14), 17, 27 (26), 33 (32), 37, 42–44, 42, 52, 52, *55*, 56
  Oberbootsmannsmaat 23 (22)
  Oberfähnrich 39 (38)
  Oberfeldwebel, Sea Reconnaissance Group 125: 39 (38)
  Oberleutnant zur See 15 (14)
  Obermaschinenmaat 7 (6)
  Oberstleutnant, engineers 49 (48)
  Oberwaffenwart 27 (26)
  parade dress 42–43
  protective clothing **12**, 27 (26)
  service dress 8, 15 (14), 27 (26), 33 (32), 39 (38), 42, 43, 44, 46, 49
  Signaloberstabsgefreiter 15 (14)
  submarine operations 20, 27 (26)
  tropical dress 22 (21), 44, 46, 48, 48, 50, 52, 53, 53
  U-Boat crewman 27 (26)
  undress uniform 43
  walking-out dress 7 (6), 33 (32), 33 (32), 43–44, **43**
  white uniforms 44, 48, 48, 49, 53
US Navy 10

weapons 25
  artillery 35, 36–37
  deck guns 13
  helmets 35, 36
  machine guns 36, 59 (58)
  one-man torpedoes 29
  rifles 35
  torpedoes 19
Weichold, *Vizeadmiral* Eberhard 52
Westerplatte 4, 17, 34
Wilhelm Gustloff 9–10, **11**
'wolf-packs' 10